MEET THE ROBISONS 6
by Bruce Robison

THE CARTERS AND THE CASHES 10
by Bill Friskics-Warren

THE EARLES 18
by Mark Guarino

THE HADENS 26
by Lloyd Sachs

CHRISTMAS WITH THE WAINWRIGHTS, THE McGARRIGLES & THE ROCHES 36
by Kurt B. Reighley

A PORTFOLIO OF FAMILY-STYLE PHOTOGRAPHS 46
by John Carrico, John Flavell, Deone Jahnke,
Erika Molleck Goldring & Thomas Petillo

THE WEBBS 56
by Peter Blackstock

THE GUTHRIES 68
by John Marks

THE SEEGERS 84
by Jesse Fox Mayshark

THE MAINESES 100
by Don McLeese

THE SONS OF REV. GARY DAVIS 114
by John Milward

THE WILLIAMSES 126
by Rich Kienzle

APPENDIX: REVIEWS 136
Neil Young, Son Volt, Joe Henry, Ian Hunter, Booker T., Larry Jon Wilson,
Wilco, A Tribute To The Songs Of Chris Gaffney.

slate

**COVER PAINTING BY
TIM SHAWL**
Gathered 'round the table at
our last supper, clockwise from
front left, are: Mother Maybelle
Carter, Bruce Robison, Natalie
Maines, Jimmy Webb, Pete
Seeger, Rufus Wainwright,
Hank Williams, Johnny Cash,
Reverend Gary Davis, Woody
Guthrie, Justin Townes Earle,
Charlie Haden, and Steve Earle.
The dog's name, of course,
is Old Shep.

INTERIOR PAGES DESIGNED
BY GRANT ALDEN FOR
NOTE OPPRESSION INDUSTRIES

Printed in the United States of America

First edition, 2009

Requests for permission to reproduce material from this work should be sent to:

    Permissions

    University of Texas Press

    P.O. Box 7819

    Austin, TX 78713-7819

    www.utexas.edu/utpress/about/bpermission.html

♾ The paper used in this book meets the minimum requirements of ANSI/NISO Z39.48-1992 (R1997) (Permanence of Paper).

ISBN 978-0-292-71930-9

Library of Congress Control Number: 2008931429

This volume has been printed from camera-ready copy furnished by the author, who assumes full responsibility for its contents.

NO DEPRESSION

the bookazine (whatever that is) #78 • fall 2009

UNIVERSITY OF TEXAS PRESS, AUSTIN

hello stranger

WHEN WE SET out to focus this 78th issue of *No Depression* (the third edition of our so-called "bookazine" experiment with University of Texas Press) on musical families, it soon became apparent that in many cases, the challenge would be to try to tell smaller stories rather than larger ones. It is, after all, an impractical task to convey the full histories of families such as the Carters and the Cashes, the Guthries and the Seegers, or Hank Williams and his descendants within the confines of a chapter, given that entire books have been devoted to them.

Still, there did seem to be some relevance in examining the sagas of those bloodlines (along with a handful of others) within the context of each other, for the sake of underscoring just how broadly the terrain of American roots music has been planted with family trees. This is not, of course, atypical or unusual; it's relatively common for children to follow in the career paths of their parents (if probably just as common for them to rebel against such pre-destinies and blaze their own trails). But the ways in which the generations have carried on, and changed, the family tradition do help us better understand the individual artists and their work.

And so, our writers sought to home in on specific aspects which helped to illuminate the way these relatives influenced one another, or shaped each other's works, or conjoined their perspectives through cross-generational collaboration. The result is a dozen passages — from profiles to essays to interviews, plus a first-person narrative and a photo portfolio — that address this matter of "Family Style" in roots music from all manner of angles.

It is, of course, ultimately just a scratching of the surface; no doubt there are dozens of other American musical clans, in varying degrees of prominence, that we could have included, absent the inevitable limitations of space and time. We considered pieces on Aretha Franklin's family, for instance, and on the influential Louisiana bunch the Savoys; the Bramletts were suggested at one point, as were the Dickinsons. Many of the pieces we did end up running might also have served as launching-points for other conversations: The Cashes and Carters could have connected to Carlene's father Carl Smith (for whom she's apparently planning a tribute album); the extended Wainwrights saga would easily have segued into a discussion of the Thompsons; and the article on the Webbs brought up the notion of a piece on Larry and Julian Coryell.

So consider this a starting-point. For our own starting-point, we turned to Bruce Robison, who was kind enough to write out some thoughts about how his family has affected his music, and vice versa. Toward the end, he notes that the everyday responsibilities of parenting can sometimes leave him feeling as if he's in "a musical family without the music" — and yet I can't help wonder what the flipside would be. What would Bruce Robison's music be like if he had no Kelly Willis to write "Wrapped" about, or if he never had musical-kindred-spirit Charlie to write "My Brother And Me" about? Take the "family" out of Bruce's musical-family existence, and his songwriting changes immeasurably.

Bill Friskics-Warren handled the daunting subject of the Carters and the Cashes with the wisdom that is typical of his work, zeroing in on their instincts toward song-gathering. It helped that Bill had interviewed both Johnny and June for feature stories back in *ND*'s bimonthly days. Mark Guarino managed the neat trick of intertwining the ties between the Earles with those of the Van Zandts, made all the more appropriate by the fact that Steve Earle's new album is a collection of Townes Van Zandt songs. Lloyd Sachs' article on Charlie Haden's family had a similarly convenient jumping-off point, in that Haden's latest album features performances by his children and harkens back to Charlie's own childhood days when his parents were musically active.

Corralling the circus that is the Wainwright/McGarrigle/Roche cross-bred cacophony would seem almost an impossible task, but Kurt Reighley found a smart entry-point by using their traditional yuletide concerts to look at how the holiday season reflects the musical exchange between kith and kin. My own observations about the Webb family across four generations centered partly on the notion that the songwriting profession in which Jimmy Webb rose to prominence is perhaps becoming as ill-fated as the old cottonwood farm on which his grandfather was raised.

The articles on the Guthries and the Seegers were perhaps two sides of the same coin, given the direct and well-documented ties between legendary patriarchs Woody and Pete. Our writers John Marks and Jesse Fox Mayshark, respectively, considered their subjects in relatively contrasting tones. Marks sought to "humanize" the Guthrie family's relationship with an American icon, reflecting upon the different ways Woody's descendants have come to terms with his legacy. Mayshark, meanwhile, opened up Seeger's legacy to a larger scope, tracing back to the early-20th-century writings of Pete's father Charles, and how those writings related to the journeys of succeeding Seeger generations.

Writer Don McLeese found that his dovetailing conversations with various members of the Maines Brothers about their father's predecessor band (and the contemporary rise of Lloyd's daughter Natalie) seemed to tell the story in itself, and so he presented it in a sort of oral-history format. The wild-card in our bunch was John Milward's piece on the metaphorical sons of the Reverend Gary Davis, which initially was assigned for the previous edition but ended up in this one when we realized it would actually fit the theme rather well. Finally, Rich Kienzle's essay on Hank Williams and his descendants was, as he described it, "significantly less reverent than my usual stuff"; given Kienzle's reputation as a keenly detailed historical writer and researcher, this one did seem like a nice change of pace for him, and provided a rather whimsical note on which to conclude things.

Some interesting threads were woven between the pieces along the way. Charlie Haden spoke of how his parents were close enough with the Carter Family that Mother Maybelle had sung songs in their living room; later in the same article, Rosanne Cash turned up with a few thoughts on her performance as a guest on Haden's latest album. Bruce Robison's ex-sister-in-law (formerly married to his brother Charlie) is Emily Robison, who is a Dixie Chicks bandmate of Lloyd Maines' daughter Natalie. And at one point during my interview with Jimmy Webb, he began singing the lyrics to Woody and Jack Guthrie's "Oklahoma Hills": "Way down yonder in the Indian nation..."

In the end, what we hope that these chapters bring to the table, even in regard to artists who have been written about at much greater length elsewhere, is specifically how the presence of music in their families affected what they have created. By extension, such examination might apply to all of us: We owe a lot more of our own stories to the foundations our forebears laid with their stories than we may tend to realize. Just as the Carters sang "Will The Circle Be Unbroken," Woody Guthrie sang (as quoted in the headline on our Guthries article) "Will The Family Be United," the title of an obscure tune filed away in the Woody Guthrie Archives. Like the Carters' "No Depression In Heaven," Woody's was a hard and sad song...but ultimately redemptive.

— PETER BLACKSTOCK

MY BROTHER AND ME, (AND THEN SOME)

BY BRUCE ROBISON

Yeah, I live in a musical family. Myself, my wife (Kelly Willis) my brother (Charlie Robison), and my ex-sister-in-law (Emily Robison) are all musicians with no other means of support. Not sure how that happened. If you asked anybody Charlie and I grew up with, I'm positive they would tell you that there was nothing then that would have pointed toward us doing what we do. Though a few years ago my brother's old friend Trey Shackleford, who is a builder now, told me he always knew Charlie and I were not gonna end up doing hard work for a living. I was a little bit irritated by that comment at the time, but not now. I think I know what he meant.

PHOTOGRAPH BY JOHN CARRICO

Our dad was a coach when we were growing up in Bandera, Texas (west of Austin and San Antonio), and we had been playing sports our entire lives. I don't think we knew anything else to do with ourselves. So we went on to play in college — me in basketball, Charlie in football — but we weren't really into it. I know I wasn't. Charlie was really good; I still think he could have possibly been a major league pitcher. He was phenomenal as a sophomore in high school, then injuries kept him from fully competing his last years, but he was good enough to get a scholarship in football despite a blown-out knee the last game of his senior year.

My sports career was stopped by lack of talent and ability. I was always playing guitar in my dorm room instead. When we were kids, my dad pushed Charlie a lot in sports, but not me so much. To his great credit, when I was in seventh grade he bought me a Fender Precision bass guitar for $250 — even though we were totally broke at the time — so me and my buddy Gerald Boyd could start a garage band. I still think that was an amazing thing for him to do. He knew there was something weird about me. I think even though he couldn't relate to me about it, he wanted to try to do something for me anyhow. It started me playing music…and I always felt his approval, though there were years I know he was worried about me and what I was doing. I hope I can do half as much for my kids.

Maybe 1988, Charlie and I got to Austin in caravan of our two old Mustangs from Arlington, Texas, where we were sharing an apartment. We had both recently washed out of college and were completely at loose ends about what to do with our lives. Charlie's car was stuck in second gear, so we drove on the access road all the way. I can't remember what our plans were. I think there was a vague notion of starting a band, but I don't think at that point Charlie even played the guitar yet. When I was in eighth grade, the drummer in our band graduated high school and Charlie got our grandmother to buy him a huge drum kit. But by the time Charlie joined, the golden era of High Voltage had already passed. Arlington was the end of that part of our lives, though I had no idea what would be next. But I know songwriter was not an option.

Austin was definitely a beacon to us. We had never lived there, but my mother's family was there, and we came at least yearly to visit. My mom's younger brother Bill was a classic Armadillo hippie. Austin was always funky and freaky and different than the rural Texas that we grew up in. Pretty soon after we arrived, we fell into the roots-rock scene around the Black Cat Lounge, the Continental Club, Hole in the Wall, etc. From that point, there seems to be a pretty direct line to where we are at today, both performing with bands and writing songs and such. I always quote Willis Allan Ramsey: We found a life to suit our style. We were sleeping late, chasing girls, playing music and workin' out who we were. As I remember, I would be talking about what I was gonna do (joining a band, starting one of my own, making a record, etc.), and then Charlie would have the guts to just go out and do it. And then that would really push me to go out and do what I was yakking about. There was always a good rivalry pushing us along; still is.

Kelly ended up in Austin roughly for the same reasons we did, but as a naturally gifted singer, her path has been a bit different from ours. She was in the star-maker machinery while we were workin' the deep fryer. She often seems a bit reluctant about the music business life that was foisted upon her. Pushing a band around the country playing in clubs is not really her idea of

they feel good at." — Bruce Robison

a good time. I wish I could sing like that. My talent was writing songs. It felt worthwhile from the first day I started. All at once, I knew how lacking I was at the things I was doing before. (And it was ten years before I made a penny at being a songwriter.) I started going to Nashville, sleeping on couches, and loving calling myself a songwriter. Still do.

In some ways, the remarkable thing about our family is how little we collaborate. Kelly and I do some shows together at the holidays, but we try real hard not to be a husband-and-wife act, just like Charlie and I refused being a brother act. We sing on each others' recordings. Charlie and I tried to make a record together awhile ago and fought for a couple days and then gave up. It was nothing serious, just what we always do. Maybe someday. It ain't the Von Trapps — though I secretly hope my kids will be more like them: singin' together, and getting along, and fightin' the Nazis and stuff. But mainly I wish for my kids that they find something they feel good at. I wonder how they will be with each other through the prism of my own siblings. (My sister Mimi is a realtor; my baby sister Robyn also is a singer-songwriter and engineer.)

My eldest son Dodie is 8 years old and he says he is going to try college but if it doesn't work out he can always fall back to being a songwriter. College is the riskier pie-in-the-sky option in his mind. I don't know what their paths will be like, but my kids' perspectives of the possibles and probables about music, and the business of it, are a lot different than mine ever were. Guess that's show biz.

Kelly and I have four kids (who does that anymore?). In addition to Dodie, there's Ben and Abby, the twins, who are 6, and Joseph, who is 3. People ask if they are musical, but who knows at this age. They take some lessons from our band members. There's lots of music around. My son Ben told me he wrote a song. I was proud and he sang it to me. It was called "Cheese And Macaronio." It was to the tune of my song "It Came

Bruce Robison and Kelly Willis at Merlefest 2004. Photograph by Grant Alden.

From San Antonio," and my first thought was, the little bastard ripped me off.

I am not sure what the kids think of it all. We go about our lives right now in a way that does not seem much different from the non-musician fortyish-hovering parents that we are surrounded by these days. Kelly and I are mostly home. She severely scaled back her workload after her last record and tour; I have been attempting to pick up the slack. But for the most part, we are able to do almost all their stuff with them and still pay the bills, which I know is incredibly fortunate. (I am writing this in a hotel in Fort Worth; I go off to play shows most weekends.) But, much of the time, being musicians doesn't seem to define us these days as much as being parents does. Sometimes that does rankle a bit, like it's a musical family without the music. But I am trying to get back to work. I have been saying that for six years.

SHOCKO GRAFIX

FRUITFUL TREE

or, "For the Sake of the Song"

HOW LISTENING SHAPED THE MUSIC OF THE CARTER AND THE CASH FAMILIES —AND BEYOND

this essay is morally good

BY BILL FRISKICS-WARREN

WE KNOW AND remember the Carter Family and Johnny Cash best for the sound of their voices, for the songs they sang and the rhythms they invented. That is, we prize them, as well as the legacies of the second and third generations of their entwined musical families, for what we've heard and continue to hear from them. This is as it should be. Taken together, the Carters and the Cashes are the closest thing country music has to royalty — eminence that, notwithstanding the iconic figure cut by the Man in Black, derives chiefly from the musical testament they've left us.

And yet for all the singing and playing they did, all the recordings and appearances, were it not for how the elders of these households listened — were it not for the songs they gleaned from others — their stories, and that of American vernacular music, might have been vastly different. And impoverished — possibly depriving the world, in the case of the original Carter Family, of the immortal likes of "Worried Man Blues," "Keep On The Sunny Side," "Will The Circle Be Unbroken," and "The Wildwood Flower," among dozens of other songs now enshrined within the canons of folk, country and pop music.

No Depression (in heaven) l. to r.: Maybelle, A.P., and Sara Carter.

Ten years ago, in an interview for a feature in *No Depression*, June Carter Cash speculated that her mother Maybelle, Aunt Sara and Uncle A.P.'s passion for finding songs — and for making them their own — might well have been their greatest contribution to the music of the 20th century. "Uncle A.P. collected a lot of the old mountain ballads as they'd come across the mountain, or from different parts of the country," she told me over the course of a stormy spring afternoon at the Cashes' home on Old Hickory Lake near Nashville. The occasion for the interview was the release of *Press On*, June's first solo album in nearly 25 years, a record that included versions of "Diamonds In The Rough" and a couple of the other songs she was talking about. "There would be people from Ireland, from Scotland, from some of those places that might have a poem, or just a piece of a poem," she went on to explain. "Somehow, they had to survive."

Not to be discounted, she hastened to add, was what her mother and her aunt and uncle did with these song fragments to ensure their survival. "My mother and Aunt Sara were great with melodies; they were great with anything they did," she said. "It was the three of them that made it the song that it was. It was a hit song because of the way my mother played the guitar or the way Aunt Sara sung or they sung together, or when Uncle A.P. came in, with his bass or tenor or whatever he happened to be singing at the time. They saved a lot of the precious music from the olden days that would have been gone forever."

Johnny Cash made much the same observation three years later, in another interview for *No Depression*. We were out at the Carter Fold, amid the hills and hollers in southwestern Virginia's Poor Valley, the rural enclave where Sara, A.P. and Mother Maybelle first encountered the songs that they turned into classics. Johnny had just finished making *The Man Comes Around*, the fourth in his series of Rick Rubin-produced albums for American Recordings. He and June were out at the old family home place working on *Wildwood Flower*, her even more Carter-centric follow-up to *Press On*. A year later, she and John — who, as she put it, were feeling "a little busted down" that morning — would be gone.

"I've always been impressed with A.P.'s work in collecting and writing these songs for the Carter Family," Johnny told me. We were sitting in the living room of the modest white cottage house, lined with box elders and Canadian hemlocks, which Mother Maybelle and her husband Eck built at the Fold during the early 1940s. "His contribution was momentous. Of course so was Maybelle's contribution, so far as writing and collecting, and Sara's.

"A.P., he went out there and was selling fruit trees sometimes, and he'd trade a fruit tree for a song. Maybe the person who wanted the fruit trees didn't have any money, but they had a song that they let A.P. have, so they taught him the song and it would wind up on the recordings of the Carter Family. He was a prolific collector. He collected everything he heard. He went all over these hills and these mountains

June Carter Cash, Press On *promotional photo.*

and these valleys around here, listening to songs and collecting different verses, and different songs from different people.

"I have followed in that tradition of collecting and writing," Johnny went on to say, matter-of-factly, although not without a glimmer of pride.

Cash was an avid student of U.S. history and folklore, and his efforts in the song-gathering department have introduced the larger public to everything from outlaw ballads, railroad songs, and the music of Native Americans to originals by such indie/alternative-minded writers as Nick Cave, Trent Reznor, and Beck. This is to say nothing of his visionary curatorial efforts while programming "The Johnny Cash Show" on ABC during the late '60s and early '70s. Over the course of its brief but influential run — it contributed profoundly to the Southernization of American culture — the TV variety hour featured guests ranging from Opry royalty such as Roy Acuff and Minnie Pearl to the cross-cultural likes of Louis Armstrong, Mahalia Jackson and The Who.

Later, the process by which Johnny and producer Rick Rubin made the albums in the American Recordings series offered further evidence of this omnivorous appetite for material. It also, as Johnny recalled during our conversation out at the Fold, harked back to the way that he and Sam Phillips used to do things at Sun Records in the 1950s. (A denim work shirt bearing the classic Sun logo was hanging out to dry on the wraparound porch of the Cashes' house at the Carter Fold that morning.)

"It was like deja vu with my Sun days when Rick said, 'Just come in, sit down with your guitar, and sing me the songs you want to record,'" he explained. "That's what Sam Phillips said. Sam Phillips said, 'Come in and let me hear everything that you like.' So I started singing my songs, Hank Snow songs, Carter Family songs, a little bit of everything.

"And that's what Rick did in 1991," Johnny continued, alluding to the record that appeared three years later, launching his career-reviving latter-day run with Rubin. "He said, 'Sit down in my living room here with your guitar and my dogs at your feet and make yourself comfortable. Let's start singing.' And that's what I did, and from those sessions, just me and my guitar, we picked an album. We must have had twenty-five or more songs."

Rubin's encouragement notwithstanding, it was remarkable that anyone, much less a member of the rock 'n' roll and country music halls of fame

Johnny Cash, photograph by Martyn Atkins.

with absolutely nothing left to prove, would still be so hungry to discover new material — much of it, on first blush, well outside his comfort zone. And yet speaking with me at the Carter Fold that morning — and despite suffering from a number of chronic and debilitating health problems — he enthused about everything from black gospel quartets to a couple of hip-hop MCs that he'd recently discovered.

"You never know where you'll find a good song, and I've always got my ears open, more so than ever," he explained. "Someone will say, 'I've got this old song,' and immediately I'll think, 'I bet I know every word of it.' They'll start in, maybe on a verse I'm familiar with, but then they'll go southwest, or then they'll go a different direction than I thought they would have gone. There'll be lyrics I never heard before, and I'll say, 'Where'd that come from?' Sometimes they can explain it to my satisfaction, and sometimes they can't."

Particularly memorable, Johnny went on to say, was the time when, out on the road during the 1960s, he met Ervin T. Rouse, the man who wrote "Orange Blossom Special." Rouse also wrote "Sweeter Than The Flowers," a song that Cash often heard growing up in rural Arkansas. "I said, 'Ervin, I've known that song since I was a little boy,'" he began. "I asked him, 'Did you write that?' And he said, 'Yes, I wrote it about my dear, dear mother who is departed.' He was a very humble man, a sweet man.

"And then I asked him about the writing of 'Orange Blossom Special.' He told me that he and his brother Gordon wrote it. Originally, it sounded like 'Talkin' Seaboard Blues.' It was that kind of thing, a question and an answer comedy kind of thing like 'The Arkansas Traveler.' But it was on a train. It was really interesting to me how 'Orange Blossom Special' got turned around to being a red hot fiddle tune here since the '60s. I've always loved the song.

"I've always been a song fan," he added, "and the songs keep coming. I heard a new song by Guy Clark called 'Homeless' [co-written by Ray Stephenson]. It's really a good song. I'm going to record it. 'Homeless, get out of here,'" he went on to sing, under his breath. "Don't give 'em no money, they just spend it on beer."

At the age of 70, and almost 12 months to the day before his death, the following September, Cash was still doing what June's Uncle A.P. had been doing, some 75 years earlier, and on the very same piece of ground: working up new material he'd unearthed. "The Carter Family was always a big influence on my music," he said, acknowledging that the ties that bound him to his wife's kin extended well beyond song-gathering.

Cash acknowledged that the Carters' "Wildwood Flower" was "one of the first songs I tried to learn to play on a guitar, and I found out I could not play the guitar. I could not play single-string stuff. I play rhythm, that's it, you know. But I wanted to play 'Wildwood Flower,'

LOOK!
Victor Artist
A. P. CARTER
and the
Carter Family
Will give a
MUSICAL PROGRAM
AT *Roseland Theater*
ON *Thursday August 1*
The Program is Morally Good
Admission 15 and 25 Cents
A. P. CARTER, Mace Spring, Va.

John Carter Cash, Johnny Cash, and June Carter Cash, 1971.

but of course I couldn't. And nobody else can. I couldn't play it, but I tried. That was one of the early influences. Of course I knew all those Carter Family songs from the time I was a kid — 'Little Moses' and 'Meeting In The Air,' one of the songs that's on [June's new] album, and 'Diamonds In The Rough.' I knew all those songs.

"I still know all those songs," he went on to say, "and musically, they were a great influence on my music. Now I'm not talking about the sound I had, or any such thing. That's all mine, and in a lot of ways it's unique. Nobody out there has done it quite like that since."

Maybe so, but listen closely to Mother Maybelle's signature thumb-brush guitar playing, where she picks the melodic line on the bass strings and strums the rhythm on the treble strings, and you just might hear the first stirrings of Cash's signature boom-chucka beat.

Such speculation aside, it's fair to say that we wouldn't have the songs of Johnny Cash, at least not as we know them today, were it not for his immersion in the music of the Carter Family. And of course we'd be without that mother lode of Americana were it not for the songs that A.P. Carter dug up and, with no small amount of help from his wife Sara and his sister-in-law Maybelle, fashioned into classics. Indeed, a case might even be made, as June did the afternoon I spent with her in the spring of 1999, that were it not for her Uncle A.P., we might not have the music of Woody Guthrie, at least not as we know it today.

No Depression (in heaven) redux: June Carter Cash and Johnny Cash, going to Jackson, no doubt.

"If you want to sing a Woody Guthrie song, I can sing you the Carter Family song where he got it," she told me. "Woody Guthrie's wife acknowledged as much at his induction to the Songwriters Hall of Fame. 'This Land [Is Your Land]' comes from two Carter Family songs, most notably 'Lulu Walls,'" June went on explain. "Woody would always write to Uncle A.P. Uncle A.P. sent him a telegram at one point and [Woody] carried it 'til it was worn out in his billfold."

And as long as we're talking about Woody Guthrie, we might also include the songs of Bob Dylan and a fair bit of what has come in their wake, including the songs of Kris Kristofferson, especially when you consider the Cashes' Carter-steeped encouragement of him. The rich

the Carter Family song where he got it." — *June Carter Cash*

and expanding catalogues of daughters Rosanne Cash and Carlene Carter are of course part of this legacy as well, as are those of John Carter Cash and Johnny & June's onetime sons-in-law Nick Lowe, Marty Stuart, and Rodney Crowell. We're talking, in any event, about an unbroken circle — one that might never have been forged had a peripatetic seller of fruit trees not kept his ears open and, on occasion, been willing to trade one of those trees for a song.

ND *senior editor Bill Friskics-Warren counts the few hours he spent with June Carter and Johnny Cash among the absolute highlights of his fifteen years writing about music.*

IF You Feel Like Lost, You'll End up Found

The Earles emerged through darkness on the edge of Townes

by **MARK GUARINO**
photograph by **JOHN CARRICO**

ineage is inescapable, the hardest truth of growing up. For children, the hints are revealed one-by-one: a certain way of pronouncing words, courtesy of mother; a funny gait, courtesy of father; or maybe how anger can blur the present moment, courtesy of someone who you never met but whose predilections they inherited from someone they never met...all these people having nothing in common except for one shared flaw that sent generations of strangers early into the ground. If genetic clues were as easily identified as the kind propping up detective novels, the mysteries of life would immediately snap into clear light.

"I went down the same road as my old man/I was younger then," sings Justin Townes Earle. The 27-year-old's natural gifts for songwriting and performing could easily be credited to his father, the vaunted singer-songwriter and alt-country politico Steve Earle. But that scenario is our wish fulfillment, not his. Despite his heritage, the younger Earle says he is defined less by the ease with which he can tap into his deep musi-

Justin Townes Earle's debut on the Grand Ole Opry. Photograph by Joshua Black Wilkins

cal roots than by how he can summon the resilience to persevere — despite the genetics of excess that invisibly plot to sabotage his every move. For him, there's no problem having to bear the Earle name, it just can be a distraction from the total story.

"I am Steve Earle's son and I have never minded being Steve Earle's son and being called Steve Earle's son," he says. "But I'm also Carol Ann Earle's boy before I was Steve Earle's son because she carried me around. My mom shaped me as a man."

Before he released his Bloodshot Records debut *The Good Life* in 2008, Earle knew he was turning down a road well-heeled by many with famous last names. What might help a young artist in getting through the first mile can become a hindrance by the second, leading to honorary detours named for horrible casualties: Julian Lennon, Lisa Marie Presley, Alexa Ray Joel.

Remarkably, *Midnight At The Movies*, his second album for Bloodshot, has quickened Justin's stride. He and his band are reaching listeners, some of whom might not be familiar with his father but are connecting to the younger Earle's sophisticated songcraft, appealing vocals, troubadour attitude and hard-rocking sound. His success has upended the affiliation with his father, making it no longer a factor, even at home.

"These days, it's turned into a funny thing: The tables have really turned, big-time," Justin notes. "My dad actually, for the first time ever in his life, very recently said, 'I have no advice to give you anymore, because this business is unrecognizable.' It's come to the point the music industry changed so much — changed before my eyes and under his nose."

As for "Mama's Eyes," a song from *Midnight At The Movies* that could be a mission state-ment issued from father to son, Earle says his father lost copies of it twice before finally taking a listen. His reaction? "Of all the things anyone can say about my father, he's always been an honest man," says Justin. "He can't argue with the song because it's a good song, and he can't argue with the facts because they're facts."

Steve Earle blazed a trail out of Nashville in the mid-1980s, becoming a different kind of country star. He had more in common with the grizzled outlaw personalities from an earlier generation than he did with the Stetson-topped hunks who would soon widen the country music industry's market share as suburbia was swallowing up the national landscape. First a songwriter for hire, Earle quickly stood out for tough road narratives, a biker attitude, and a weary but indignant voice that sounded punk — components that left many choking dust on Music Row, but somehow helped Earle brandish an authentic, if sort of cranky southern voice with ambition as vast as Bob Dylan.

He found a mentor early: Townes Van Zandt, a cowboy poet invisible to most people except die-hard admirers, including fellow songwriters who recorded Van Zandt's songs. The music world is filled with pretenders who profess a vagabond recklessness in their press bios and House of Blues dressing rooms, but Van Zandt was real. He kept the dark side close at hand as he drove his songwriting into the deepest waters of human mysteries, resurfacing with material of remarkable purity. In May, 12 years after Van Zandt's death at age 52, Earle channeled his gratitude into a single album: *Townes*, a full-length collection of Van Zandt covers.

"It felt right because Steve's apprecia-tion of Townes is a unique one; he kind of picked up the torch when Townes died," says John Townes Van Zandt, 40, the elder's son. "His appreciation and love of Townes is so unique. I'd be a little suspect of anyone who announced that type of project; I think he's definitely the right person to do that."

John Townes remembers Earle running with Townes, who was eleven years older than Steve, in Houston, back when their group included fellow musical miscreants Rodney Crowell and Guy Clark. Tagging along as a

Steve Earle (l.) and Townes Van Zandt. Photograph by Jim Herrington.

pre-teen, J.T. remembers being left alone outside his grandmother's house for a few minutes with Earle, who ended up fumbling with a BB gun and taking out the windshield of a parked car.

"We joked in the car and floored it," John Townes says. "It's one of those memories I have

John Townes Van Zandt. Photograph by John Carrico.

that sticks out how reckless and lawless it was back then. But no one was showing signs of the damage. Steve still looked like the picture on [his 1986 album] *Guitar Town*, and Townes was still handsome and strong. They were kind of the glory days."

In years to come, as Earle became Van Zandt's most outspoken promoter, Townes became a kind of surrogate father for Steve, sharing the role of Jack Earle, the family patriarch, whose lifelong love affair for music made an impact on his children (and, later, his grandchildren). Singer-songwriter Stacey Earle, who was introduced to the business through her older brother, said she remembers her parents pointing the family car in one direction and then driving there strictly for the purpose of leading group sing-alongs.

"That's where their stage was," she says. "My dad loved to drive. He drove every inch of North America in his station wagon just to see how far the station wagon would go, with no plans except to keep driving until he had to be back at work."

Jack Earle worked as an air traffic controller, but in earlier days he sang in a barbershop quartet, and was known for his tenor voice and a love of performing that was contagious to everyone close to him. Even when Steve started running away from home as a teenager, from Houston to Nashville, his father gave up retrieving him and instead started showing up in town — not to throw his son in the car, but to sit back and listen to what he'd been up to.

"Dad was our biggest fan; he was everyone's biggest fan," Stacey says. "A lot of people in the music industry knew who Jack Earle was. When Steve was playing coffeehouses when he was a teenager, my dad was maybe one of five people sitting in the audience with [guitar] strings in his pocket."

Steve (who declined interview requests) told National Public Radio in December 2008 that his father's decision to let him go instead of locking him down helped to reinforce his confidence at a critical age of his musical development. "Nobody in my family, even on my mom's side, ever discouraged me from playing music," he said. "Because...I was a really messed-up kid. I got in a lot of

Stacey Earle, late 1990s. Photograph by Frances Wong.

trouble really fast, and when people saw me taking interest in something, and it looked like I might be kind of good at it, people started going, 'Please, do whatever you've got to do.'"

there was not a lot of emotion to it." — Justin Townes Earle

Jack's enthusiasm for supporting his family's musical pursuits extended in his later years to the hardcore punk/metal played by Kyle Mims, Stacey's 27-year-old son. Kyle plays drums with a Jacksonville, Florida, band called Evergreen Terrace. Mims says his grandfather was "very important," and remembers Jack and Barbara Earle, his grandmother, attending various Evergreen Terrace shows in Nashville – an unlikely sight in "a little club with people going crazy, jumping off things and killing each other." But his grandparents "bought our T-shirts and really soaked it up....They were in the back of the room with a big grin on their faces, watching."

Jack died of a heart attack the day after Christmas in 2007, and there are still tremors from the loss. "Dad was always there for everybody," says Stacey. "My parents were very young at heart; they loved the whole thing and they never turned anybody away."

Jack Earle at Merlefest, 1999. Photograph by Grant Alden.

Considering that Jack Earle served as such a focal point for his family, his death compounded the fragility between his children and grandchildren. With Steve Earle having relocated from Nashville to New York after his 2005 marriage to singer-songwriter Allison Moorer, communication has become a delicate process, one that has been worked out in music, in the press, but not always face-to-face.

Justin Townes Earle did not find music directly through his father, who lived on the other, better side of town. Instead, the younger Earle was raised on hip-hop and metal until age 12, when he discovered Nirvana. "That changed my perception of music pretty quick," he says. Kurt Cobain led Justin to Lead Belly and other pivotal folk and blues figures, but the discovery coincided with his introduction to his father's music — the result of being asked, at age 12, by his stepmother to move into Earle's spacious home in Fairview, half an hour west of Nashville. By then, Earle was a commercial star, but he was simultaneously dealing with serious heroin abuse, and circling the family wagon was considered a way to perhaps help get him sober.

At that time, Justin did not know his father, who divorced his mother when Justin was a toddler. Moving from Nashville's urban ghetto — where his mother worked a rotation of manual jobs — to his father's more comfortable setting did not necessarily guarantee a father-son reunion in full bloom. "I don't know what the thinking was there," Justin recalls. "I don't know what I was thinking. I was a kid who thought his dad was going to die. I must say, there was not a lot of emotion to it. It was like, 'OK, I'll do anything.'...I hated living in Fairview."

The home not only sheltered Justin, but also Stacey Earle and her son Kyle, as well as others who had been invited to move in so they could remain close. However, as months passed and Steve returned from long stretches of touring or recording in Los Angeles, he would retreat into deeper abuse.

At her brother's invitation, Stacey sang backup vocals on Steve's first world tour. She also quietly started writing her own songs, which would eventually spark the folk-music career she now shares with husband Mark Stuart. But back then, while guitars and other musical equipment were common sights in Earle's house, so too were guns and drug paraphernalia. Coming back from the tour for Steve's 1990 album *The Hard Way*, Stacey realized "he was pretty sick."

Guy Clark (l.) offers Justin Townes Earle a quick lesson in capo management, at Merlefest 1999. Photograph by Grant Alden.

"It took me awhile to really see it," she recalls. "After we got home from tour, I saw it unfolding day-by-day and decided, 'I have to get me and the kids out of the house.'"

Justin bounced around between living with his stepmother, his father, and his mother. "I was an angry teenager for a pretty long time," he says. "All teenagers hate their fathers at some point. I had a bona fide reason to hate my father, and it took me a long time to realize it wasn't worth that." Many fathers and sons might have separated for life after that, but Justin says music provided the connector which prevented that from happening. "Pretty much everything we had was built off of that," he says.

At age 14, driven by Nirvana's *MTV Unplugged* album (which included covers of hallmark folk and blues songs), Justin felt a transformation taking hold. "Those old songs really meant something," he says. "So I literally dropped out of school…and I locked myself into the basement of my dad's house with an ounce of pot and started listening to Lightnin' Hopkins and Mississippi John Hurt while [my father] went on the road. He was away for a month and my whole world changed. I was listening to Mississippi John Hurt [before], but I learned how to play Mississippi John Hurt."

Almost immediately he started writing songs, some of which appeared over ten years later on *Midnight*. When his father returned home and heard his son's expert fingerpicking and songs taking shape, he took interest. "We had something to talk about finally that was on an even playing field," he says. Eleven years later, on *Townes*, father and son trade vocals on "Mr. Mudd & Mr. Gold," the Van Zandt song that Steve played for Townes when they first met in 1972.

t he genetic lineage that the musicians in the Earle family share is not confined to a flair for performing. According to Stacey Earle, past generations of her family have struggled with excessive alcohol and drug abuse, inclinations that her epilepsy helped control. "Probably, if I was not epileptic I would be an addict. It probably saved my life," she says.

While Steve's struggles are now a part of his official biography and a source of some of his greatest songs, Justin's are less-known but no less harrowing. He's been sober for four years now, but he started experimenting with hard drugs when he was 12. When he was 22, he wound up in a hospital, nearly dead from respiratory failure after being high for fourteen days in a row. Changing course not only meant alleviating the body's dependence on drugs and al-cohol, but also determining where the line between art and the romance in making art is drawn.

"A lot changed when I quit getting high, when I quit drinking and quit living this bullshit fucking myth," he says. "I've always been a very honest songwriter, but the problem in the past was, *I* wasn't honest. I had to get honest in order to be an honest songwriter."

That realization also helped him to better understand his father's situation, including the reasons for his extended absences during Justin's youth. "My father was a touring musician, so no matter if he was a junkie or not, he wouldn't have been there," he says. "That's the way the business works. I'm not pissed off about that shit anymore."

John Townes Van Zandt is probably one of the few who can understand. He was 28 when his father died, and he says he went through a long period of self-pity before he came to terms with the "tremendous amount of literary work" his father left him and his younger brother and sister, which gave them insight on how to continue their lives.

"My dad was much better at writing about the essence of human existence than acting it out," he says. "So if I separate my dad the writer from my dad the father, I can compare the two and I know where he went wrong. I think without my father's music, I would have made the same mistakes that he did."

John Townes came to admire his dad for his "fearless-ness," even if it prevented allowing him a normal childhood. "He shaped his entire existence in a way to produce the best songs he possibly could. Nothing was an accident, even the suf-

Justin Townes and Steve Earle. Photograph by Joshua Black Wilkins.

fering he brought upon himself. Basically he sacrificed any safety net that you need to find out what that place was."

Mark Guarino writes regularly for The Christian Science Monitor, Chicago Tribune *and* Chicago Sun-Times. *His full-length play* All The Fame Of Lofty Deeds, *based on the music and artwork of Jon Langford, will be produced by the House Theatre of Chicago in November 2009. More of his work is available at www.mark-guarino.com.*

THE SHAPING OF OZARKS

Jazz great Charlie Haden's music spans the American century, from his parents' country radio show to Ornette Coleman's harmolodic improvisations, and back.

by Lloyd Sachs
photograph by Jacob Blickenstaff

THE

"Mother Maybelle Carter sang songs and told stories in our living room.

Yes, it's a long, long way to Tipperary. But it's not exactly a hop, skip and jump to Los Angeles from Shenandoah, Iowa — especially if, as Charlie Haden did in chasing his muse, you factor in a significant detour to New York City. We're not concerned with the miles the great bassist has traveled as much as the worlds he has bridged in beaming himself from the farmland setting of *Little House On The Prairie* to the big-city shadows of *The Long Goodbye*. What were the odds of two-year-old Cowboy Charlie, who yodeled his way into heartlanders' hearts on "The Haden Family Radio Show," growing up to embrace the stuff that jazz dreams are made of?

And that's not the end of it, either. What were the odds of Haden, five decades after finding himself on the ground floor of Ornette Coleman's harmolodic jazz revolution, returning to the hillbilly music of his youth — with his own grown son and triplet daughters and second wife in tow? When Charlie recorded *The Shape Of Jazz To Come* with Coleman in Los Angeles at age 21, could he have anticipated releasing *Rambling Boy*, the acclaimed 2008 country album by Charlie Haden Family & Friends, at age 71?

Charlie, whose family moved to Springfield, Missouri, when he was 4, says that returning to his musical roots on *Rambling Boy* wasn't that big a stretch: "This stuff is always inside me. It never leaves." Neither do the Ozarks, as he demonstrated on *Beyond The Missouri Sky*, his Grammy-winning 1997 album with guitarist and fellow Missourian Pat Metheny, which featured Roy Acuff's "Precious Jewel." Two of Charlie's albums with his Los Angeles band Quartet West, which mostly draws its inspiration from postwar Hollywood film noir, also cast an eye back on his rural past. *Quartet West* (1986) includes "Taney County," a solo medley of country ballads dedicated to his parents, while the richly atmospheric *Haunted Heart* (1991) features him singing "Wayfaring Stranger," a folk tune his mother sometimes sang.

Still, when Charlie went to Nashville to record *Rambling Boy*, it had been a lifetime since he played that music. He was nervous about working with country stars including Vince Gill and Ricky Skaggs, keeping up with a cast of bluegrass virtuosos, and perhaps finally realizing a longstanding dream. "He was working toward this album, consciously or unconsciously, his entire life," says his son Josh Haden, a singer, songwriter and member of the indie-rock group Spain (and, like his dad, a bassist). He was, that is, working back toward the Ozarks. Working his way back to the farm.

Geography's grip on style is one of the great fascinations of American music. One wonders: Would great Texas tenors such as Illinois Jacquet and Arnett Cobb have developed such big, spacious sounds if they had grown up in the closer confines of, say, Kansas City? Would Count Basie have developed his supremely economical style as a pianist and bandleader had he come of age as an artist not in hustling and bustling K.C., but the rural south? What musical path would little Bruce Springsteen have followed had he grown up in Tulsa, or Elvis in Garden City, Long Island? Henry James said you didn't have to visit a place to write about it. Can you also "play" a place you haven't been to?

Growing up among future farmers of America, little Charlie seemed a likely candidate

I fell in love with Anita. I was 9 and she was 15." — *Charlie Haden*

for a life in country music. As the legend goes, he made his debut at 22 months on his family's radio program on 50,000-watt KMA in Shenandoah after impressing his mother Virginia by humming in harmony with her lullabies. The Hadens serendipitously had landed the KMA job before Charlie was born when a snowstorm forced them to stay in Shenandoah on their way to Des Moines. Charlie's father, Carl, had traveled all over performing on radio shows since the early 1930s, first as part of Carl & Ernest and the Missouri Hillbillies, then with Virginia as Uncle Carl & Mary Jane.

In Springfield, with children in the frame, Uncle Carl and the Haden Family appeared every morning on KWTO ("Keep Watching The Ozarks") from their farmhouse near Charlie's grandmother's home. Charlie got up at 4 a.m. every day to milk the cows and feed the chickens before doing the show, along with his older siblings Carl Jr., Jim and Mary. Carl was friends with such luminaries as Hank Williams, Jimmie Rodgers, the Delmore Brothers and the Carter Family, who became regular visitors after a network barn dance show patterned after the Grand Ole Opry called "Korn's A-Krackin'" began attracting Nashville artists.

Charles Edward at age 3.
His newest picture, cowboy boots and everything,

"Mother Maybelle Carter sang songs and told stories in our living room," says Haden. "I fell in love with Anita. I was 9 and she was 15. She was beautiful. When she started playing bass it was like, man oh man, that's it."

But however powerfully such early surroundings — and early crushes — imprint themselves on an artist, the creative heart can still want what it wants, to steal Woody Allen's memorable utterance. Exposed to his brother Jimmy's jazz records, Charlie caught the jazz bug early. A trip to Chicago with his father in 1948 to attend Don McNeill's Breakfast Club, one of the most popular radio shows of its day, had a decisive impact on the small-town kid. "The noise of the city thrilled me," he says in *Charlie Haden: Rambling Boy*, a new film documentary by Reto Caduff. The noise of a 1951 Jazz at the Philharmonic concert in Omaha, Nebraska, featuring Charlie Parker, Lester Young and Billie Holiday, thrilled him even more.

Singing with his family, Charlie developed an appreciation for pure harmonies and melodies. "My dad was a musical disciplinarian," he says in the documentary. "He made sure we always sang in tune and blended well." But the deeper Charlie got into jazz — a direction Carl Haden was not thrilled about — the more he wanted to leave the friendly confines of country: "I loved complex harmonies. The further out they were, the better I liked them."

And the more he was exposed to jazz musicians, particularly after a case of polio damaged nerves in his throat, ending his singing career at 15, the more he wanted to trade in his small-town existence for the life of a jazz player. When Charlie was 13 or 14, his father took him to a concert by Stan Kenton's band in Springfield, where they met some of the musicians and were invited back to their hotel. "I knocked on the door," Haden recalls. "When it opened, all this smoke came pouring out. I never smelled anything like it. There were guys in their undershirts drinking whiskey saying, 'Here, Charlie.' My father said, 'You really want to be a jazz musician? Look around the room.' I did, and said, 'Yeah!'"

After landing a house job playing bass on "The Ozark Jubilee," a network TV show in Springfield (hosted first by singer Red Foley with country-jazz guitarist Grady Martin in support and then by singer Eddy Arnold with the innovative jazz-leaning guitarist Hank Garland in the band), Haden was on his way. It was just a matter of saving up money to go to the west coast, which he did, on a Greyhound bus, in 1956.

Growing up in Los Angeles in the 1970s, living with their mother after their parents' divorce, Charlie Haden's kids were exposed to very different sets of influences and personal circumstances — and songs — than their old man had been as a boy. But however different they are, generationally speaking, music is as crucial to Josh and the triplets, Petra, Rachel and Tanya, as it is to their parents, and was to their grandparents. Though Petra says she once thought about becoming an astrologer, neither she nor her siblings ever gave any serious thought to not pursuing a career in music.

Their mother, Ellen Haden, a therapist in Los Angeles, also comes from a musical family. Her parents were members of the Los Angeles Mandolin Orchestra. She was "a huge musical influence on us kids growing up," says Josh, who was 7 when his parents split in 1975; the triplets were 4. "She made sure my sisters were all taking music lessons and taught me about all kinds of music from a very early age. She was always very encouraging to us musically, and still is."

Josh, who left his mark on *Rambling Boy* with his brooding "Spiritual" (a Jeff Buckley-like song from Spain's 1995 album *The Blue Moods Of Spain*, subsequently recorded by Johnny Cash on *Unchained*), grew up listening to modern and classic jazz. Friends of his father including Keith Jarrett, Don Cherry, Dewey Redman and Metheny were frequently around. Metheny gave him his first guitar when he was 13. "Josh was singing Keith Jarrett songs when he was 3," says Charlie.

But as depicted in family photos of him at age 5 with headphones on, intently listening to the Beatles' *Revolver*, Josh became more devoted to rock. As a pre-teen, he was a passionate follower of hardcore punk bands including the Minutemen, Black Flag and the Meat Puppets. "I don't know why I veered away from the strict idiom of jazz," Josh says. "Maybe it was because I had my own voice to find." This was, he said, fine with his old man (who may well have gotten a charge listening to Minutemen bassist Mike Watt).

Petra's projects have included an electronically involved a cappella recording of *The Who Sell Out*, mock commercials included, and an offbeat recording of standards and covers with Americana-minded jazz guitarist Bill Frisell. As a violinist, she has toured with the Decemberists and recorded with artists ranging from Beck to the Foo Fighters to Victoria Williams.

Rambling at Lincoln Center, August 25, 2008 (l. to r.): Tanya Haden Black, Rachel Haden, Petra Haden, and Charlie Haden. Photograph by Jacob Blickenstaff.

Petra and Rachel, a bassist and pianist, were members of That Dog, an indie-rock band which released three albums in the '90s. Tanya, a cellist and visual artist, is married to *School Of Rock* star Jack Black (who contributes a manic reading of "Old Joe Clark" to *Rambling Boy*) and has recorded with Los Angeles band the Silversun Pickups, among others.

As his kids developed their own distinctive styles, Haden took pains to keep them tapped into their family history. He frequently played them old tunes over the phone, though without ever pressuring them to play them — or to play any music professionally. "I wanted them to be in touch with their grandparents and their cousins and uncles," he says, speaking from his home in Agoura Hills, California, outside Los Angeles.

When the Haden kids were asked to harmonize on "You Are My Sunshine" with relatives at an 80th birthday celebration for Charlie's mother Virginia in Missouri in 1988, no one knew quite what to expect. Though the triplets had a great time harmonizing with each other when they were young, swapping harmonies and competing for the high parts, they hadn't sung much country. Like his father, Charlie is a musical disciplinarian. "He can be pretty critical," Tanya told an NPR interviewer. "He knows when he likes something and when he doesn't."

Happily, the sing-along, orchestrated by Haden's future wife, the singer Ruth Cameron, was a success. "I knew how great they were," says Charlie. "They all have really great ears. Petra has perfect pitch. All these kids have perfect pitch. But I had never heard them do country. The way they blended was phenomenal. I loved the way they sounded."

Cameron, who became Haden's longtime manager and co-producer as well as his spouse, credits the singing at the party with motivating Charlie to eventually make his country album. Whether or not it would have happened anyway, as Petra and Josh believe, is a moot point. *Rambling Boy* is a reality, and Cameron, in addition to contributing "Down By The Salley Gardens," a vintage number derived from a William Butler Yeats poem, played a significant role in seeing it through to fruition. "Just getting the names of all the artists on the front cover was an achievement," she says. And there's more to come, with at least one Haden Family live performance slated for the fall of 2009.

Cameron, who recorded the 2000 standards album *Roadhouse* with her husband, revealed she had a pressing reason for wanting him to undertake *Rambling Boy*. "Charlie had been suffering from pneumonia a lot," she explains. "I wanted him to do this project as a family legacy." For a fellow known to be fidgety about his daily health, that angle no doubt added a bit of intensity to the death ballads.

Nashville portrait, clockwise from the top: Josh Haden, Ruth Cameron Haden, Petra Haden, Tanya Haden Black, Charlie Haden, and Rachel Haden. Photograph by Jim McGuire.

When the Haden clan traveled to Nashville to record *Rambling Boy*, they hooked up with yet another tradition-steeped family of sorts — a prolific crew of session all-stars who frequently work together, including dobro player Jerry Douglas, fiddler Stuart Duncan, mandolinist Sam Bush and singer-mandolinist Dan Tyminski.

They all were featured on the T Bone Burnett-produced *O Brother, Where Art Thou?* soundtrack, which perhaps paved the way for *Rambling Boy* and many other country-roots albums by raising the profile of American mountain music and the Irish and Scottish traditions from which it emerged. Charlie was not familiar with Burnett and didn't know what he contributed to *O Brother*: "Does he play?" Charlie asked. But he was acutely aware of Tyminski through his rendition of "Man Of Constant Sorrow" on the soundtrack. "That's why he's on [my] record. I had to have him," he says.

Any nervousness Haden felt about recording *Rambling Boy* quickly faded. "He went ahead and does what he does, what his parents did every night: organizing the music and performing it," says Cameron.

In honoring the music of his youth, including songs by the Carters, Hank Williams, and the Louvin Brothers, Haden hardly tossed the past six decades overboard. *Rambling Boy* is not the purists' delight that the 1930s-rooted, period-sounding *O Brother* was. Not with Metheny applying his pastoral jazz voicings as player and producer, on tunes including the instrumental

recording, and when it works, it's transcendent..." — Rosanne Cash

"Is This America? (Katrina 2005)." Not with another of Haden's good friends, Bruce Hornsby, asserting his gospel and blues sensibility on vocals and piano. And not with Elvis Costello singing Williams' "You Win Again."

"As we got closer and closer to the project, I found out that the rediscovery of Charlie's roots wasn't really what it was gonna be," says Jerry Douglas. "Pat [Metheny] brought in another, completely different feel. There were two records, really."

Haden asked Costello to record "You Win Again" with him for *Rambling Boy* after seeing him perform it on his cable program, "Spectacle: Elvis Costello With...," the same night that Haden and Metheny appeared on the show along with Bill Clinton. Two days after the taping of the show, Haden and Costello were joined in a New York recording studio by Metheny and guitarist John Leventhal, husband of Rosanne Cash. She got drafted as well for a Haden arrangement of "Wildwood Flower," an old staple of Mother Maybelle's that Charlie's mother had sung on the radio.

Nashville Cats in the big city (l. to r.): Vince Gill, Charlie Haden, Sam Bush, and Jim Mills at Lincoln Center, August 2008. Photograph by Jacob Blickenstaff.

Rosanne knows a little about making music with family — the drawbacks as well as the rewards. "You try to work out your deepest emotional conflicts either onstage or in a recording, and when it works, it's transcendent and it changes both of you," she says. "When it doesn't work, it entrenches you further in the conflict. When my father invited me to sing with him the last time he played Carnegie Hall, I went onstage with a rock of resentment in my gut, which he was well aware of, and I came off with only the love. I've gone onstage with my husband angry and self-righteous, and come off infused with the grace of the music we created together. I don't know about Charlie. It seemed he was perhaps past all that. It seemed easy and inspired. But of course you never know the back story when it's not your family!"

For Stuart Duncan, Haden's song choices were as unexpected as the jazz arrangements. "I thought, wow, this guy goes way deeper than I expected," says the native Californian, who like many bluegrassers cut his chops on jazz. "I had never heard some of these songs." They included "Fields Of Athenry," an old Irish folk ballad featured in the Cate Blanchett film *Veronica Guerin*; "20/20 Vision," recorded in the 1950s by bluegrass giant Jimmy Martin; and Walter T. Adams' "Rambling Boy."

"Charlie collects a tremendous amount of music, and keeps a lot of it in his head," says Cameron. "All of a sudden, he'll come up with something." And he has multiple outlets for the songs: Quartet West for jazz standards once sung by the likes of Billie Holiday, Jo Stafford and Jeri Southern; the politically minded Liberation Music Orchestra for Central American and Spanish folk anthems; a full array of trios and duos for blues and ballads. In the end, his remarkable voice on the double bass — or, if you prefer, bass fiddle — unifies his music. It's a voice of special pleading, big and vibrant and eerily resonant. One Nashville musician called it "otherworldly."

To understand Charlie's unusual presence in Nashville, you have to understand the time-keeping role that jazz bassists played for so long, and in many or even most cases play still. One of Charlie's early heroes, Ray Brown, who performed with Charlie Parker at that 1951 Omaha Jazz at the Philharmonic concert, was known as Father Time for his impeccable pulse. Haden's notes have so much hang time, to use basketball parlance, they can seem to ignore bar lines, scoring emotional and tonal points more than rhythmic ones. In country and bluegrass, where the time function is so crucial, you never hear a bassist playing the way Haden does on *Rambling Boy*. "He can brush a string and hold it for three beats until he gets to a note," says Duncan, who first encountered Charlie on Metheny's 1980 double album *80/81*. "I've never heard stuff like that before." For Duncan, Charlie's approach brings to mind the legendary Bob Moore, onetime "Ozark Jubilee" bassist, who perfected the art of "flopping the beat."

At the Rambling Boy sessions, "Charlie stuck to his guns," says Douglas. "He played the way he always does. He didn't cut off notes. He let 'em ring one into another. Only other guy I worked with a lot who pulls that out is Viktor Krauss. Jerry Scheff also had a big old sound like Charlie's."

Asked about the connections he makes between jazz and country, Haden has described jazz as a music created by poor black people and country as a music created by poor white people. Would it be an overextension of our family theme to view him in the greater context of the family of man? There are few borders he hasn't crossed, musically or geographically, and few human rights causes he hasn't pleaded, through the sustaining, proselytizing force of his notes and through political protest. In 1971, while on tour with Ornette Coleman, Charlie was arrested in Portugal for dedicating a song to Angolan rebels. The title of the most recent Liberation Music Orchestra album, *Not In Our Name*, was taken from the antiwar protests leveled at the Bush administration by Americans.

Haden is no Pollyanna. He has been shaped as an artist not only by the rich harmonies and sweet melodies he grew up with, but also by the dark themes contained in the songs put forth by Uncle Carl and the Haden Family. His father may have signed on with a cheery, "Good morning, good morning, everyone everywhere," and the theme song of the show may have been "Keep On The Sunny Side Of Life"; but as jazz critic Francis Davis has pointed out, "nothing else they sang was as cheery." In a profile of Haden in *The Atlantic*, Davis characterized "Wayfaring Stranger" as a song "whose grim lyrics, accepting death as a prelude to the afterlife, are typical of the songs Haden performed on the radio as a child."

Charlie has a vivid memory of his mother taking him to an African-American church in

until he gets to a note." — Stuart Duncan

Thank you and good night: Curtain call at Lincoln Center, August 2008. Photograph by Jacob Blickenstaff.

Springfield when he was 9. "We sat in the back row and listened to the choir," he recalls. "Man, I loved those spirituals." Years later, he would channel that moment on *Steal Away: Spirituals, Hymns And Folk Songs*, his remarkable duo album with the venerable jazz pianist Hank Jones.

When Cowboy Charlie looks back on his life, he remembers a bunch of entertaining details, including the albums his brother didn't want him listening to and the products his father pitched on the radio, like Wait's Green Mountain cough syrup and Sparkalite cereal. What he feels from the past, in his bones, is the sense of togetherness, and wholeness, with which making music with his family filled him. It's a two-way street. On *Rambling Boy*, he pays tribute to his parents, and the past, most movingly with his patchy but heartfelt vocal on "Shenandoah." At the same time, he celebrates the bright future of his own children.

"Music is always something that brings us closer together," says Petra. "It makes us feel good." Can there be any doubt it will bring the next generation of Hadens closer together as well? The odds, to say the least, are with them.

Lloyd Sachs, a writer based in Chicago, dedicates this article to his own departed mother and father, and to the late Jacques Lowe, a famous photographer who kindly took a snapshot of Sachs and Charlie Haden with Sachs' poor excuse for a camera at the 1996 Umbria Jazz Festival.

MERRY CHRISTMAS
The holiday season offers a focal point for the clan connections

BY KURT B. REIGHLEY

PHOTOGRAPH BY TIMOTHY S. GRIFFIN

FROM THE FAMILY

between the Wainwrights, the McGarrigles, and the Roches

IT MUST BE HELL MAILING OUT CHRISTMAS CARDS WHEN YOU'RE A WAINWRIGHT.

Start with singer-songwriter Loudon Wainwright III. Marriages and children immediately link him to two other great folk families, the McGarrigles and the Roches. The natural tendency of musicians to flock together introduces even more characters into the fold. The resulting network of relations and friends is a show business dynasty that rivals the Carter and Cash clan in breadth.

And like the annals of most artistic broods, the Wainwright saga is full of notorious episodes. Infidelities and divorce. Drug addiction and recovery. Peaks of fame and troughs of obscurity. The stuff soap opera scribes — to say nothing of confessional singer-songwriters — thrive on.

Yet that sensationalist take is only one possible perspective. Forget the blood, music, and backstage drama for a moment. There is another thread that binds the Wainwrights, McGarrigles, and Roches together, one that has endured through all the marriages, birthdays, and that damn "funny animal song." If you want to better understand some of the forces that make this family tick, look at how its members behave at Christmas.

LUCY WAINWRIGHT ROCHE, the daughter of Loudon Wainwright III and Suzzy Roche, en-

tered the world to the sound of Christmas music. The day was December 16, 1981. "My mom was actually singing carols on the sidewalk when she went into labor," discloses the singer-songwriter.

It was probably inevitable. The New Jersey trio of sisters Maggie and Terre and Suzzy Roche first garnered attention performing carols a cappella in the New York subways. By the time Lucy was born, the Roches had gone above ground; they'd cut two albums for Warner Bros., and worked with Paul Simon and Robert Fripp. But the spirit of the season, instilled in them by their mother, still ran high in their veins. Come December, they would round up friends and hit the New York streets to carol.

Lucy Wainwright Roche with her lovely pink guitar. Photograph by Heidi Ross.

They were warbling away on the corner of 53rd Street and 5th Avenue when it happened. "Normally we would sing on the fly, put out a hat, and make a run for it before the police showed up," recalls Suzzy. Back then in NYC, the boys in blue didn't cotton to random acts of holiday cheer, even if the public did. "That particular day, a cop came by to stop us, and the crowd got angry at him, saying things like 'Why don't you go arrest some criminals and leave these carolers alone!' It was quite a scene."

In the midst of the hubbub, Lucy made her entrance. "It was at that point that I doubled over in contractions," Suzzy says, "which made the poor officer's job even harder." After the delivery, while mother and daughter rested up in the hospital, Loudon brought Suzzy a cassette of the Cambridge Boys Choir to keep their spirits high.

The years that followed afforded Lucy abundant opportunities to lift her voice in song come December. The Roches released a Christmas album, *We Three Kings*, in 1990. Their popular holiday programs at the Bottom Line were an annual tradition throughout her childhood. "When I was very little, I used to sing carols in the Christmas shows," she says. "The first time I did it, I was 4. I got up onstage and started crying. My dad had to come up and take me off."

Lucy watched as her half-siblings Rufus and Martha — the children from Loudon's marriage to Kate McGarrigle — began writing and performing music of their own. "Though I grew up very much with the Roches, I was never disconnected from any part of [the family]," she explains. But she

Maggie and Suzzy and Terre Roche, in a festive mood. Photograph by Irene Young.

had no inclination to follow them into the family business. So much so that, when holiday parties or celebrations turned into a sing-along, she refused to join in.

"The guitar would come out, and we'd say, 'Come on, Lucy...,'" remembers Loudon. "And she would kind of walk out of the room."

"I didn't mind being around it, and having other people do it, but for many years I did not want to participate," she confirms. "I didn't want to sing. At Christmas parties, I would always refuse." Her father, who stopped living with Suzzy when Lucy was young, but remained close, was not amused.

The irony is that Loudon — whose latest album, a two-disc exploration of roots-music pioneer Charlie Poole, features guest appearances by Martha and Rufus as well as the Roches — expresses his own reservations about group singing. The Brooks Brothers suits and cropped hair he sported when he began performing in the late '60s weren't the only thing that distinguished him from his peers in the Greenwich Village scene. "I'm kind of a stage hog," he admits. "Hootenannies were not my idea of a good time. Even when I do folk festivals now, I hate that last song where everybody has to get up there and sing 'Kumbaya' or 'We Shall Overcome.' I only do it because I don't want to be rude."

Previous spread: Martha (l.) and Rufus Wainwright celebrating the holidays at Carnegie Hall, New York, December 20, 2008.

Unlike Lucy, Loudon had something of an excuse. Although both he and his younger sister, Sloan Wainwright, would go on to become performers, he didn't grow up with a kitchen or living room full of musicians — at Christmas or any other time. Music was not a family pastime. "My Dad played a few piano chords, and wrote a few damn good songs, actually, but we didn't sing together," Loudon says. "My mother could not carry a tune, in fact. She could not sing 'Happy Birthday.'" As a young man growing up in Westchester County near New York City, Loudon wasn't especially keen on Christmas either, as anyone who has listened to the stark original "That Hospital" (from 1995's *Grown Man*) has probably already deduced from the second verse: "Now my dad freaked out and he wound up there/One Christmas way back when..."

"My father actually had a nervous breakdown at Christmastime," says Loudon, frankly. Some folks look forward to stringing garlands of popcorn and cranberries, and mulling wine, and singing carols. And others don't. "In my experience, there's not a lot of middle ground," he says.

On the other hand, his sister Sloan — who hosts Christmas shows of her own — takes refuge in the songs of the season. "I have always loved the music of the holidays — from traditional and religious carols to Chuck Berry and Joni Mitchell," she says. "Seasonal music has always carried me through, helping with the oncoming darkness of winter and the chance to begin again with the New Year."

The Roches definitely fall into the pro-Christmas camp, too. And during the years Loudon and Suzzy cohabitated, following his split from Kate McGarrigle in 1976, he slowly came around. "I lightened up a little more about it," he admits.

Loudon Wainwright III, 2007. Photograph by Michael Traister.

"Oh yes, Loudon was very Scrooge-like," says Suzzy. It made for some "raucous" seasonal dust-ups, she adds. "But he'd only resist right up until the few days before, and then he'd cave, get a tree, run out and buy some slipper socks for everyone and we'd even wind up throwing a party.

"Loudon is very sentimental and sweet, with a heart of gold," Suzzy continued. "He's just a fierce social commentator, so sometimes those elements collide." One need look no further than the words to Wainwright's "Christmas Morning," written for one of those early Roches Christmas shows, to see what results from those collisions. The song, which eventually appeared on his 1999 album *Social Studies*, juxtaposes images of skaters at Rockefeller Center with asides about homelessness, AIDS, and political turmoil in the Middle East.

"I'll never forget when he came over to play me the song," Suzzy remembers. "It was so depressing and sad that we howled laughing till tears fell out of our eyes." He would also fix his sights on how opening day for the Christmas shopping season now falls immediately after

darkness of winter and the chance to begin again...” — Sloan Wainwright

Halloween (“Forget about Thanksgiving, it’s just a buffet in between”) for the equally pointed “Suddenly It’s Christmas.”

In 2005, the Roches revived the Christmas show tradition, staging a holiday to-do at New York’s Town Hall. Lucy, who’d previously been earning her living as a teacher, had spent the past summer touring as a backup singer with her half-brother Rufus. Now the bug had bitten her, too, and she stepped into the spotlight, alone, for one of the first times in her nascent entertaining career. The New York Times singled her out for mention: “When Lucy Roche...sang ‘In the Bleak Midwinter,’ her voice’s power and purity melded her parents’ best attributes.” Not bad for an artist who hadn’t even created a MySpace page yet. Since then, Lucy Wainwright Roche has released a pair of eight-song EPs. In their simplicity, they are as different from her father’s biting, autobiographical oeuvre as they are from Rufus’ operatic swooning and half-sister Martha’s bluesy art songs. She has performed with Neko Case on “Late Night With David Letterman,” and swapped verses of “Come A Long Way” (a song written by Kate McGarrigle) with John Wesley Harding at the Doug Fir nightclub in Portland. Like Rufus and Martha before her, she started out supporting her dad on tour, then graduated to headlining dates of her own.

And now, when the guitar comes out at social gatherings, Lucy takes her turn. “Once you start doing it professionally, you can’t really get out of it at parties, without being sort of disingenuous,” she admits.

Sloan Wainwright. Photograph by Nicholas Marwell.

IN 2005, THE SAME YEAR Lucy won raves for her turn in the Roches’ Town Hall holiday spectacular, Kate & Anna McGarrigle issued *The McGarrigle Christmas Hour*. It was a sequel of sorts to their 1998 release, *The McGarrigle Hour*. Like that disc, which included performances by extended family and famous friends on a program that featured originals side-by-side with standards, the *Christmas Hour* found the first ladies of French-Canadian folk joined by Rufus, Martha, and Anna’s daughter Lily Lanken, plus Emmylou Harris, Beth Orton, and Teddy Thompson, for a bill of seasonal favorites and a sprinkling of new tunes.

Even though their parents divorced when they were small, childhood Christmases were joyous for Rufus and Martha Wainwright. “That time of year has always been very pleasant, and not filled with anxiety, as it can be for other families,” says Martha. It helped that the setting was in the snow-covered Laurentian Mountains, north of Montreal, in the house where Rufus and Martha’s mother and aunts were born. There was a big family dinner, and a living-room fire. "We've always had this idyllic and fantastic Christmas," Martha remembers, "which is no doubt why we eventually made a record."

In Loudon Wainwright III's childhood home, the Christmas music was left to the Bing Crosby and Ella Fitzgerald albums that came out once a year. The McGarrigles took a much more D.I.Y. approach — after the turkey and pie, that is. "Food was the main focus, to be honest," says Martha. "But after meal time, then came carols. And that was something that probably came from my mother and my aunt's own experience with their parents."

Frank and Gabrielle McGarrigle played piano and sang popular songs. They made sure their daughters Kate, Anna and Jane were all versed in the musical arts, too, right down to singing three-part harmony. "That was a family activity, as it probably was in many other families," says Martha. And it was passed down to the next generation, including the emphasis on polyphony.

"I know that my mom really enjoyed taking the opportunity to challenge us," recalls Martha. A quick pass through "Jingle Bells" or "Frosty The Snowman" wasn't going to cut it for the McGarrigle sisters or their kids. "When it came to Christmas carols, she would find things that were in three- or four-part harmony," Martha says. "So we'd read music, and look at things on more of a classical bent." That predilection for Old World-style carols informs *The McGarrigle Christmas Hour*, too; the stately "Il Est Ne Le Divin Enfant" and the hymnlike "Seven Joys Of Mary" are hardly staples of quickie Christmas cash-in albums.

On those occasions when they left Montreal and visited their father in New York during the holidays, young Rufus and Martha also got to sing with the Roches, both at the Bottom Line and on the city streets. "I remember once a 6-year-old Martha sang with us and charmed the crowd,

without knowing one word of any Christmas carol," recalls Suzzy.

"That was definitely an eye-opener for me, because I found that I really enjoyed being onstage," says Martha of those visits. The Roches' take on the holiday music canon wasn't quite so formal, either. "It had a little more of a sense of humor, a different approach. They made caroling exciting, and for a young girl, that was exactly where I wanted to be."

The ability to sing together, in small combos or large ensembles, continues to serve all the family members well, not just the McGarrigle sisters and the Roches. When Lucy supported Rufus on some California dates in May 2009, Loudon — who now lives in Los Angeles with his wife Ritamarie and their 16-year-old daughter Alexandra — got up onstage to run through his own "Needless To Say" and the cowboy

Martha Wainwright. Photograph by Mark Squiares.

song "Old Paint" with them one night. In the summer of 2004, Kate, Anna, Rufus, Martha and Lily all toured the U.K. together.

"When you're singing with a group, the most important thing is the sound of the group, rather than one individual in it," says Martha. "Hopefully, I have learned to really strive for that sound that happens when the harmonics and vibrations are just right. It is something

then came carols." — Martha Wainwright

that is very close to a religious experience, because it is one that becomes very physical. It literally resonates. That's what group singing is about."

Every member of the extended Wainwright family is a singular vocalist. Sloan Wainwright possesses an earthy alto imbued with a gravity that rivals Odetta's, while Martha can put audiences on the ropes with her heightened flights of emotional vulnerability. Rufus loves opera and Judy Garland. Lucy covers Crash Test Dummies and Fleetwood Mac.

"We all sound different, which I think is a real blessing," says Lucy. "And that's great, because you don't want to be too similar to anyone else. That's why it's worked for everyone to be doing their own thing; we don't get in each other's way too much. There's a lot of variety within what's happening."

"It's an asset because it's authentic," concurs Sloan Wainwright. Especially when they share a bill. "During the course of an evening of music, our differences and our connections as family create a powerful experience," she says.

Put two or more of them onstage together, and something in those disparate instruments clicks. "I don't know if it's because of genetics, but certainly in the case of my family, the meld of the voices is very good," says Martha. "Although individually the voices might sound quite different, somehow

Rufus Wainwright, 2003. Photograph by Yelena Yemchuck.

in the combination it makes a lot of sense, and doesn't clash." Their relations may not have always been harmonious, but they know how to harmonize.

THERE IS ANOTHER TRADITION IN THE Wainwright family that has been passed down

between generations: composing autobiographical songs that reference family history. Given Loudon's extensive catalogue of entries — "Rufus Is A Tit Man," "Pretty Little Martha," "Dilated To Meet You," "Hitting You," "Your Mother And I" — it comes as less of a surprise that Rufus ("Dinner At Eight"), Martha ("Bloody Motherfucking Asshole") and other family members have engaged in the practice, too. Martha and Loudon even poked fun at it on the duet "Father-Daughter Dialogue."

"It is true to say that there certainly has been dialogue through music in the family, for better or for worse," admits Lucy. "It hasn't bothered me, to the extent that it's involved me at all. I guess I really didn't think about it much as a kid, since that's just the way that it was."

"Merry Christmas And Happy New Year," Martha's original contribution to *The McGarrigle Christmas Hour*, is a lesser entry in this subgenre. But it merits mention because a) so many family members pop up in the lyric, and b) it ultimately shows how the dialogue can take on a positive tone.

"Like a lot of my early songs, I was really seeking to describe my life in my music," remembers Martha. "And I used a lot of family themes, because that is something that weighed heavily on my mind, certainly during the holidays." Written over a decade ago, Martha imagined the rest of the clan celebrating — Kate cooking dinner for "twenty of Rufus' L.A. friends," Loudon and Lucy hanging out in New York — while she was stuck in southern New Mexico, shooting a student film.

"It was actually a very joyful Christmas," she hastens to add. "I was just trying to encapsulate in the song the experience of being away from your family, and wishing them happy holidays, wherever they are."

Lucy cocked an eyebrow when she first heard "Merry Christmas And Happy New Year." "My Dad has a song where my name is mentioned specifically, but it doesn't happen that often, so I definitely noticed." She's more interested in what, if anything, outsiders might take away from such personal details in any of her relatives' work. "It's always interesting when songs are very specific, what it sounds like the person is saying to other people, who are not in the family."

And of course, writing a song that mentions your children, spouse, siblings, or parents, and dissecting all the gory details for the press afterwards, are two completely different things.

"My feeling is you write what you write," says Lucy of the creative process. "It's better to not censor yourself." The after-the-fact commentary, however, can benefit from judicious filtration. "It's fun to read about people talking about their songs, but not everybody has to have all the information about what exactly you meant. Especially if it might hurt somebody's feelings."

SINCE 2005, THE MCGARRIGLE Christmas shows

have — pun intended — snowballed. There have been three concerts at Carnegie Hall. In 2006, there was supposed to be a whole McGarrigle Christmas tour, but

Kate (l.) and Anna McGarrigle. Photograph by Diane Dulude.

Kate fell ill, which nixed most of the gigs. But not all of them. In New York, Rufus and Martha served as hosts; out west, Loudon and the Roches covered the Los Angeles date.

In December 2009, members of the family are bringing "A Not So Silent Night" to London's Royal Albert Hall. But regardless of the venue or seating capacity, Martha says the spirit of their ongoing Christmas productions is still very much rooted in the home-and-hearth tradition of those Canadian family celebrations past.

"We do all the planning ourselves," Martha says. "It is very folky, and very much an exten-

like our family works the best." — Lucy Wainwright Roche

sion of [what we do]." Kate McGarrigle knitted the background used in the promotional posters herself; in 2008, she baked 800 cookies for inclusion in the gift bags of VIP-level ticket holders.

There is the glitzy side of the production to consider, too. *The McGarrigle Christmas Hour* album and the original 2005 show hewed pretty close to what a casual fan might expect in terms of a talent roster — i.e. heavy on the roots and folk-music crowd. The involvement of Rufus' "best friend" Teddy Thompson — son of Richard and Linda Thompson — roped a whole other storied folk clan into the affair. Lineups in later years have cast a wider net: Laurie Anderson, Lou Reed, and even comedian Jimmy Fallon have augmented the ever-widening circle of Wainwrights, McGarrigles, Lankens, and Thompsons.

"Even though some of them are famous, and we would've wanted them there for obvious reasons — to fill the room — they are truly and utterly great friends, and kindred spirits," says Martha of their invited guests. "And they 'get it.' Right away, with the rehearsals starting and the whole process, there is a professionalism, but it is also very familial."

That extended family includes transgender and gay performers, too. And not just Rufus. In 2006, Antony of Antony & the Johnsons fame put his distinctive stamp on "Blue Christmas." Singer and performance artist Justin Bond tells a hilarious anecdote of how, backstage at the 2008 show, he and his accompanist, Our Lady J — both self-proclaimed "tranny witches" — introduced Emmylou Harris to the age-old cross-dresser's trick of pushing back flab forward, to create bigger cleavage.

"It's not a United Colors of Benetton thing; nobody thinks that way," Martha acknowledges. But diversity, and the notion that family is defined by things besides blood and marriage, are definitely among the things being celebrated. "Artists are people who sometimes feel estranged from society, as can gay and transgender people," Martha says. "Hopefully, by having people from all walks of life, we're creating another family, a family of friends, too. And perhaps that can inspire people to feel that way about their neighbors."

Making room for everyone at the table, elbows and all, is what allows the Wainwright brood to coexist in relative peace the rest of the year, too, suggests Lucy. "Overall inclusion is the way that a complicated situation like our family works the best," she says. "Everybody is 'in.'" The moment anyone starts trying to change that is when things go south, she adds. And then she laughs quietly.

"The human race is like that as well. It's better if everybody is just allowed to be."

Kurt B. Reighley is a Seattle based writer, DJ and entertainer. He is currently working on Frontierland, *a book about youth culture's fascination with trends from bygone eras. Although he has composed numerous songs about boyfriends, and even a few Christmas ditties, he has thus far had the good sense to leave his family out of things.*

FAMILY STYLE

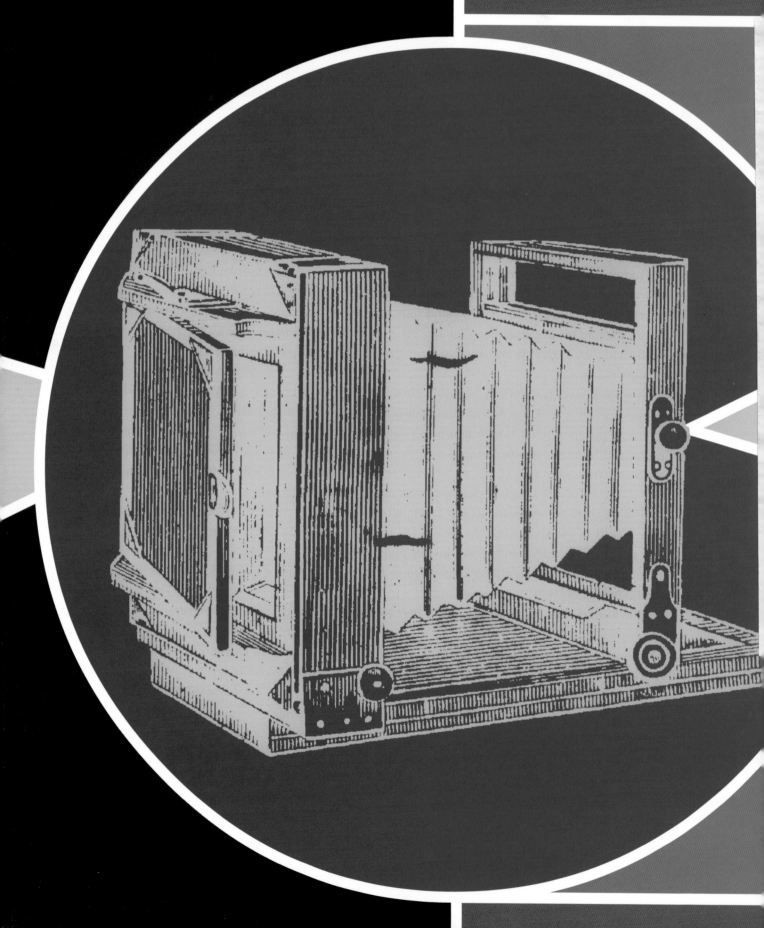

PORTFOLIO

VARIATIONS ON A THEME IN NO PARTICULAR KEY BY JOHN CARRICO, JOHN FLAVELL, DEONE JAHNKE, ERIKA MOLLECK GOLDRING, & THOMAS PETILLO

SHOCKO GRAFIX IN HOMAGE TO ALEKSANDR RODCHENKO

ABOVE: *Ricky Skaggs (in the background at right, wielding a Nikon D200) photographing his son Luke, left, while soundchecking for the Skaggs Family Christmas Show, December 16, 2006, at the Paramount Arts Center, Ashland, Kentucky. Photograph by John Flavell.*

ABOVE: *The Felice Brothers at the Newport Folk Festival, August 2008, obliged to go all acoustic by a storm which knocked out the electricity. Pete Seeger was in no way responsible. Photograph by Erika Molleck Goldring.*

LEFT: *The Wooldridge Brothers (l. to r., Scott and Brian) at Turner Hall, Milwaukee, Wisconsin, May 2009. Photograph by Deone Jahnke.* **ABOVE:** *The Itinerant Locals (Zac, Cheryl, Eureka, and Zephyr), at home in Hot Springs, Arkansas. Their website is polkayoureyeout.com. Photograph by Thomas Petillo.*

ABOVE: *Billy Joe and Eddy Shaver on an outdoor stage in Austin, Texas, during SXSW '95. Photograph by John Carrico.*

ABOVE: *Doug and Shawn Sahm at the Austin Music Awards, Austin, Texas, early 1990s. Photograph by John Carrico.*

ABOVE: *The Del McCoury Band (l. to r. Rob, Ronnie, and Del) at the 40th annual New Orleans Jazz & Heritage Festival, New Orleans, Louisiana, April 2009.* **RIGHT:** *Joseph Pierre Boudreaux (Big Chief Monk Boudreaux) with Mary and his grandaughter Nucie, heading out to meet the rest of the Golden Eagles, New Orleans, Louisiana, February 2008. Photographs by Erika Molleck Goldring.*

DO WHAT YOU GOTTA DO

Jimmy Webb's kids couldn't help but follow him into music, even as it became a more difficult road to travel. Now they're sharing the journey together.

by PETER BLACKSTOCK

photograph by JESSICA DASCHNER

"…you know, I would write the best piece of music I've ever written, and then

Where have they gone, don't they ever walk
Don't they ever slow down, don't they ever walk
I used to think his eyes were melting
Gazing at the constant weather
But now I know, he cried sometimes…
— Jimmy Webb, "Cottonwood Farm"

"It was almost a divine intercession, that this piece of music was really meant for this purpose," muses Jimmy Webb, discussing the title track to *Cottonwood Farm*, the new album in which he collaborated with the Webb Brothers — his sons Christiaan, Justin, James, and Cornelius. Though "Cottonwood Farm" was written more than 30 years ago, Jimmy never released it; the only recording in existence over the decades was a solo vocals-and-piano demo, which clocked in at a shade past ten minutes.

It's an epic composition, even by the standards of the songwriter whose seven-minute opus "MacArthur Park" remains one of the longest songs ever to hit the upper reaches of the *Billboard* charts (via the late Richard Harris in 1968, and again ten years later with Donna Summer's disco remake). It's also, quite possibly, the best thing he ever wrote — even acknowledging that this is the guy responsible for "Wichita Lineman" and "Galveston" and "Highwayman" (among hundreds of other songs covered by an impossible range of artists).

One of his foremost peers thought so, at least. "Paul Simon once told me, 'This is the best piece of music you've ever written,'" Jimmy relates. "And I thought, well, yeah, it probably would be, because, you know, I would write the best piece of music I've ever written, and then I wouldn't record it for 30 years. That's what I would do."

He chuckles at the folly of that reality, then turns more philosophical. "Even though I didn't know it at the time, this album is the reason that I wrote this piece of music. Because it was really the glue that brought our family back together again, after a pretty nasty divorce, and some rough times as a family. It's been a real healer for us."

Jimmy Webb clutching a fresh song, 1997. Photograph by Carolyn Jones.

Cottonwood Farm, due out this fall on Proper Records in conjunction with a November tour of the United Kingdom, is indeed a full-on family affair. It teams Jimmy not only with his offspring — who, as the Webb Brothers, made a fair name for themselves in recent years with a few indie-leaning pop albums — but also with his father, who contributes vocals to "Cottonwood

I wouldn't record it for 30 years. That's what I would do." — Jimmy Webb

Farm" and takes a solo turn on the mid-20th-century standard "Red Sails In The Sunset," a song that looms large in Jimmy's memories of his childhood. "I can remember my father singing 'Red Sails In The Sunset' to me," he says, "literally sitting on his knee, with him and his guitar, watching his fingers."

Jimmy gives considerable credit to his parents, Robert and Sylvia Webb, for fostering his musical development during his childhood years in the 1950s in the small Oklahoma town of Elk City. "I grew up in this incredibly musical family," he says. "My father played guitar; my mother played accordion. He was a Southern Baptist minister; music was a weekly affair, like it was for J.S. Bach, who wrote cantatas nonstop. And we learned at a young age to carry a tune. We learned to sing harmonies, to get up in front of a group of people. When you think about it, it's almost like a laboratory for creating performers. We learned to stand up in front of the whole church and sing, and make mistakes, and keep going.

"It was my mother's dream that I would be the pianist for the church by age 12, and I was able to do that, due to her unfailing sense of discipline. When I did not have much discipline, she had a lot. She'd put the egg timer on top of the piano and set it for 30 minutes, and say, 'OK, when the bell rings, you can go outside.'"

His father and mother had performed for awhile, along with an aunt and uncle of Jimmy's, in a group called the Buffalo Quartet. "They went around and played local gigs in that area of southwestern Oklahoma," Jimmy says, recalling that they played songs such as Rex Griffin's "Won't You Ride In My Little Red Wagon" and Woody Guthrie's "Oklahoma Hills." "The piece de resistance was 'Old Shep,'" Jimmy laughs about one of the chestnuts in his father's repertoire. "He would do 'Old Shep,' and all the women would cry, and all the kids would cry. I can remember people saying, 'Robert, do "Old Shep," do "Old Shep!"' And I can remember Mom saying, 'Robert, if you do "Old Shep," I'm leaving!'"

His parents' musical endeavors and encouragement provided the foundation, but Jimmy built on it when he began doing something different: writing original songs. "It started during the offertory at the Southern Baptist church, when they would pass the plate along the aisle, and I had to think of a way to fill twenty minutes or so with something approximating an interesting musical presentation," he says. "I would begin to do variations and different chord changes, and customize the hymns that were available into some kind of musical program. That was the germination of the improvisational skills that really are the primary tools of the songwriter."

Webb's development from that point is relatively well-chronicled. Not long after his mother's death in the early 1960s, he decided to try to make it as a songwriter. He headed for Los Angeles and hooked up with folks such as Johnny Rivers who helped him get his songs in front of hitmaking singers and performers. By the end of the decade, he'd written chart-toppers and received multiple Grammys — heady stuff for a guy who was barely into his 20s.

Webb took a different approach in the 1970s, seeking to establish himself as a performer and recording artist as well as a writer. Though the five solo albums he released during the decade weren't big sellers, today they stand as artistic landmarks of an era which produced

"I kind of got into playing piano, and {dad} was very cool

a handful of genius-level songwriters recording for labels such as Reprise and Elektra and Asylum. "Guys like Mo Ostin at Warner Bros., Lenny Waronker, people like that, almost ran a laboratory over there for strange musical types, like Van Dyke Parks, Randy Newman, Leon Russell," Webb recalls. "It was kind of a freaky bunch of people sitting around, waiting for their turn to go in and talk to the bossman."

Webb's steady recording output (he released four albums between 1970 and 1974) began to slow in the mid-1970s, in part because he'd begun to raise his own family. His 1977 album *El Mirage* included the song "Christiaan No," named for his first son; around the time that album was released, Jimmy's second son, Justin, was born. Three more boys followed over the next ten years — James, Cornelius, and Charles — and then finally a girl, Camilla, who just finished high school this past spring. All but Charles and Camilla appear on the new *Cottonwood Farm* album.

Inevitably, it seems, the Webb children have been swept into the slipstream of music, if by varying degrees and measures. It started with the oldest two. "Christiaan and I have lived totally parallel lives," Justin says. "We had bunk beds, and then we shared an apartment in college, shared flophouses and rehearsal spaces in Chicago — you know, everywhere, we just were always together, until a couple years ago." (Justin, who got married this past spring, lives in Southern California, as do brothers James and Cornelius; Christiaan has lately been back and forth between California and Missouri, where his fiancee's family is from.)

It was Christiaan who took to music first.

The Webbs who made the album, (l. to r.): Christiaan, James, Jimmy, Cornelius, Justin and Robert. Youngest brother Charlie isn't on the record, but snuck into the photo behind his grandpa. At far right are drummer Cal Campbell and pedal steel player Tim Walker. Photograph by Jessica Daschner.

"Christiaan, from the time he was 8 or 9 years old, he was like, 'I'm gonna be a star,'" Justin says. "He had bands, he had music videos that he shot on my dad's camcorder in the backyard. He's always been a real dreamer."

For his part, Christiaan remembers "trying to write songs, totally intrigued by watching my dad, the way he played piano and the way he wrote. I got kind of into playing piano, and he was very cool about encouraging me, and buying me new synthesizers and stuff."

Justin was a different story. "We were very close as kids, but he was also very private about his music," Christiaan explains. "He'd play his guitar in the attic and no one knew what he was doing up there....We didn't start playing together until college. He had a little tape of some songs he was writing, and I realized that this is the guy I wanted to write songs with. It was kind of a revelation, because I'd been making music without him for so many years, and here he was, quietly writing these songs and playing guitar."

Justin offers further insight. "I was kind of like an Alex P. Keaton kid," he says. "I was really conservative — not like [politically] conservative, but just conservative in my decision-making; very pragmatic, and very practical. I was into songwriting, but I didn't see it as a practical long-term career.... It really took Christiaan and his spirit of risk-taking and optimism to drag me out of my solitary closet songwriting

All of these LPs, among hundreds of others, contain at least one song written by Jimmy Webb. Photograph by Peter Blackstock.

place, and to say, 'You're good, and you can do this, and we can do this together, in fact.' He's really the one that took me out of my shell, because I wouldn't have taken those kind of risks."

Their father was supportive but not pushy. "I didn't take an active role" in steering them toward music, Jimmy says. "But they had a propensity for it, and they grew up around it, and they always thought it was pretty neat....They also had kind of on-site training. They went to gigs, they had pianos and instruments laying around the house, they had recording equipment they could use. There was an inexorable kind of force that pulled them in.

"And I watched it happen with mixed emotions, because I thought, oh God, this is going to be rough on them. There's going to be a lot of 'up' moments, and those are going to be great, and then there's going to be some 'down' moments. And I'm going to be there for all that — because I'm the dad."

Christiaan and Justin's musical partnership began during their brief tenure at Boston

to drag me out of my solitary closet songwriting place..." — Justin Webb

University, where Christiaan had a band Liquid Courage that eventually evolved into a new outfit called Mercybeat which included Justin. At some point they met street-singing indie-pop sensation Mary Lou Lord, who recruited the brothers as backing musicians for an opening-slot gig with Guided By Voices. Christiaan recalls the experience as formative in redirecting their outlook on music.

"She was the one that turned us on to that band, which became such an influence on the Webb Brothers and really made us kind of redefine ourselves as 'indie' musicians," Christiaan says. "Whatever that meant, we wanted to be that — as far as breaking out of our childhood influences, and, whatever my dad had exposed us to, and then whatever we saw on MTV....Maybe it was growing up around so many famous people and stuff; it makes you a little self-conscious about going into the music business. Meeting those people made me feel so much more at ease, and made me feel like I could just concentrate on my craft."

Shortly thereafter, the brothers moved to Chicago, where eventually they gave into the obvious notion of billing themselves as the Webb Brothers. It wasn't that they had been shying away from associating themselves with their father's name; well, not entirely, anyway. "We didn't wanna be riding coattails," Justin allows; "we were maybe a little too aware of that at the time. But also, we were kind of transforming from bands to bands. Members would come and members would go, and basically, by the time we started calling ourselves the Webb Brothers, we didn't have a band anymore. You know, our band was sick of following us from dirty club to dirty club and not making any money. It had basically dissolved."

Jimmy Webb, 1978.

Looking back, Jimmy expresses some regrets about their departure from school, but he acknowledges the circumstances that played into it. "Chris and Justin took that plunge pretty early and decided, well, screw college, we're goin' for it....All of a sudden they just decided, well, this is what they were gonna do. There was some trouble at home, there was a divorce brewing, and, I think they thought, 'We'll do it. Because Dad did it, we can do it.'

"And, you know, that has always kind of bothered me, because the paradigm of my success was, I run away from home when I'm 17, basically, and I go to Hollywood, and I have a couple of rough years, but at the end of that, I get Grammy Awards. That's disturbing to me, because, if they thought that was going to happen to them, the odds of that happening are astronomical."

"I think he was concerned," Christiaan acknowledges, "and looking back, rightly so." Still, the brothers didn't necessarily believe they would, or even could, follow in their father's footsteps. "The songwriter as an occupation that it was in the 1960s didn't exist when we came out," Justin observes. "So you couldn't really follow in his footsteps, for a number of reasons. It was impossible to re-create what he did. And so, we just did whatever seemed cool to us at the time musically."

"When I get out there, I've got a lot to sing for. I've got everybody

And then a funny thing happened: The Webb Brothers' career began to take off. With the help of their childhood pal Julian Coryell — the son of noted jazz guitarist Larry Coryell, who was good friends with Jimmy — they made a record in 1998 called *Beyond The Biosphere* that earned them a deal with the U.K. division of Warner Bros. A second album, *Maroon* (which was released in the U.S. as well as overseas), received critical accolades and led to tourdates with

some big-name acts in the U.K. A third, self-titled album, on an independent label, followed in 2003 before things essentially stalled.

"They almost made it happen in their young years," Jimmy marvels in retrospect. "They came very close, in a very antipathetic record business — a business that was a lot rougher and a lot more difficult than the one I grew up in. I mean, they had to sell a certain number of records to stay on the label, and if they missed that number, they were off the label. I was never up against that; I made record after record after record that didn't sell."

In the end, Christiaan figures his dad felt "a certain amount of pride in what we did.

The Webb Brothers, in triplicate (l. to r.): James, Christiaan, and Justin. Photograph by Jim Newberry.

We could actually support ourselves with music for years, and travel the world, and make albums and stuff....And to tell you the truth, working on this album with him now, I think, oh God, I'm so glad we had all that experience — because I actually feel like that experience was almost necessary to feel comfortable with this."

Midway through the Webb Brothers' run — after they'd recorded *Maroon*, but before they began touring behind it — Christiaan and Justin brought James into the fold. James was just short of earning a degree in music at Bard College when he left to join the band, a decision that remains a sore point for Jimmy but with which James seems to be at peace. "He's a good enough pop to let me make my own decisions, my own mistakes," James says. "Whether or not that was a mistake, I don't know. I can still knock out a string quartet and a woodwind section faster than anybody else."

One point James underscores is that he was inspired by both his father and his brothers. "My dad was one thing — and he was a great, successful songwriter — but my brothers, I really looked up to them too. And I saw that they had a degree of success, and I figured I'd just start walking down that road and something would happen for me, eventually."

Musically, James is perhaps more like his father than any of his siblings. "My thing was, I wanted to get out there and do Van Dyke Parks-style arrangements," he says. "I wanted to really stand out. It wasn't necessarily important for me to have a conventional band in any way. I knew that I wanted to be able to create different musical environments with arrangements."

in my family to sing for; I've got my whole life." — James Webb

That's largely what led him to Bard, where he was in "basically a conservatory program," he says. "I'd taken three years of composition, three years of musical theory, three years of vocal repertory. I was sort of in boot camp for music. I was priming myself up to be prepared; I wanted to be really good at arranging strings and woodwinds and horns."

And one other thing: singing. "The three years of vocal repertory really taught me the nuts and bolts," he says. "I learned to sing like a classical singer; I got a lot of powerful exercises and understanding of the mechanics of the human voice. And it helped me enormously."

One of his best vocal lessons, long before conservatory classes, came from attending Jimmy's performances over the years. "I've watched him perform all my life — he's a big influence on how I approach the whole thing, absolutely," James says. There's a similarity in the way the two men throw caution to the wind in their vocal delivery, and James realizes the importance of drawing upon such emotionalism for the collaboration with his dad.

"I feel like I've gotta go crazy on this one," he says. "When I get out there, I've got a lot to sing for. I've got everybody in my family to sing for; I've got my whole life. If I want to be a musician, I've gotta sing my guts out, so that it's as good as it can be. And then, if it doesn't happen, I can look back and say, well, it wasn't because you were a subdued performer!" He laughs. "So when we get onstage, I'm not nervous, but it's high stakes. It's very high stakes for me."

Unlike his three older brothers, Cornelius Webb actually did finish college, earning a degree from the Conservatory of Music at SUNY-Purchase, a state school just north of New York City. Cornelius (the family calls him Cory) is playing bass in the family band; he says he's also "a pretty solid drummer," though on *Cottonwood Farm* the drum seat was filled by another old son-of-a-family-friend, Cal Campbell (whose dad Glen has recorded more Jimmy Webb songs than any other artist).

Cornelius' band experience is more limited, though he did do some Webb Brothers gigs in the latter days of their run. The chance to play with both his brothers and his father clearly is a thrill for him, if also a bit daunting. "He's my dad, but he's also one of the greatest songwriters ever, so it's a privilege to be able to play with him and have that opportunity," Cornelius says.

"It's got me reading again; some of Dad's stuff is so complicated that I just had to have it on notes in front of me to figure it out. When we go out to England, we're going to try to do 'MacArthur Park' — which I really want to do, because I figure it would just be so much fun live, if you actually got it off and the whole band was cookin'. But all those transitions — I think the song has, like, 45 chords in it. But that's kind of the fun part of playing with my dad, is that he brings that element into it — that serious modal-jazz and classical element, and the virtuosity of his instrument. I'm a solid bass player, and my brothers are good songwriters, but none of us are virtuosos on our respective instruments in the way that my dad is. It's definitely been a challenge playing with him."

It's likely also been somewhat of a challenge for Jimmy, who rarely has played anything other than solo piano gigs in the past couple of decades. "For my dad, it's a whole new thing to be playing with a band, which is something that he hasn't done for a really long time,"

Cornelius says. "And he's getting a big kick out of that. Because it really changes things. Like, he can't stand to play things the same way twice, so you always really have to be paying close attention to him, and watching him when he's playing. Because he'll just change things on the fly. He'll drag out a bar an extra measure or two, or slow it down, just with the emotion he's feeling at that moment. Little things like that can make a big difference.

"He kind of considers himself to be a transcendentalist, and he really has an artistic and spiritual connection with his music. You can see it when he's playing — he's closing his eyes, and it's about the music and the songs, and he really feels it. That's something that I'm also taking from this project, and playing with him — he's really investing so much emotionally into the performance, and the expression of it."

One of the bigger challenges in making a "Jimmy Webb & the Webb Brothers" album was choosing material to be included. It was settled early on that the record would consist of approximately half Jimmy Webb songs and half Webb Brothers songs (the latter batch being a mix of tunes from Justin, Christiaan and James). In addition to "Cottonwood Farm," a couple others from

Jimmy's catalogue surfaced as clear choices. "Highwayman," a smash for the country supergroup of Willie Nelson, Waylon Jennings, Johnny Cash and Kris Kristofferson, was ideal for divvying up the four verses between Jimmy, James, Justin and Christiaan. And "If These Walls Could Speak" (covered over the years by Amy Grant, Nanci Griffith, and Shawn Colvin) struck a chord because of its personal relevance to the family.

There was a conscious effort to steer away from the big hits; though they'll play some of those songs live, on the album they gravitated toward lesser-heard numbers from the Webb songbook, including "Where The Universes Are" and the previously unreleased "Snow-Covered Christmas." Part of the plan, says Justin, was, "How do we expose the world to the best Jimmy Webb songs that aren't really common knowledge?"

The Webb family. Photograph by Jessica Daschner.

Though the song-selection process was ultimately "democratic" — "we all voted," says James, "and whichever songs got the most votes went on" — it was Justin who helmed the project. "Justin is a natural-born administrator,"

to the ebb and flow of fate, as artists." — Jimmy Webb

Jimmy says. "He grabs the reins of power instinctively and begins to formulate a plan." He's also become quite accomplished in production, Cornelius contends: "He's got a lot of attention to detail in what he does. I mean, he's a great songwriter, but he's become a world-class editor as well in the last couple years."

Producing the album is not something Justin has taken lightly. "It's a lot of responsibility," he says. "The music is so good, and you want to try and make, you know, if not the definitive version, a great version....And with 'Cottonwood Farm,' I really want to try and make the definitive version. Just to get my grandpa, and his soulful, honest voice on it, while he's still around, is just priceless."

The character at the center of "Cottonwood Farm" stretches back another generation beyond the Webb Brothers' grandfather. The song is about Jimmy's grandfather (on his mother's side), who passed away in the mid-1970s. It's a remembrance of simpler days in rural Oklahoma, a time of church-going and cotton-growing, of milking cows and fishing holes, of Sunday-morning radio programs and picture shows in town, of forts and caves and Indians and monsters.

When Jimmy wrote it in the early '70s, his grandfather was still alive. "Yeah, I played it for him several times," he says. "I remember one time in particular; he had retired from the farm and was living up on the river, and had a pretty little place in the dunes there, and still had a garden out behind his house. He could never stop growing things. But, he sat in a chair, and there was this old upright piano nearby, and I played it — 'Raised a family, broke his back, always drove a Pontiac' — and the tears just began to roll down his face. It was a great moment, but in many ways it was a very tough moment. It was tough for both of us."

The final lines of the song bid an aching farewell to those old ways:
They cut the trees and they plowed down the cotton
They dammed the river and they broke its arm
Old times there are not forgotten
Just lost in dreams...

What his grandfather lost in the wake of those changes — what he could no longer pass on to his children and grandchildren — is perhaps, in some ways, analogous to what Jimmy is losing in his own day and age. In terms of self-sustenance, the profession of music is quickly becoming a fallow relic, its bounty cut and plowed, its conduits dammed and broken. And yet the dreams...the art, the craft, the creative spark that sets it all alight...are not forgotten. Sometimes the music must be its own reward.

"Agnes DeMille said, 'There is no satisfaction, only a divine dissatisfaction,'" Jimmy Webb concludes. "Which is a quote that I guess I should have stuck on my icebox. That's what it is: It's a divine dissatisfaction. It is connected to a higher source. And we just have to, in a way, submit ourselves to the ebb and flow of fate, as artists."

ND co-editor Peter Blackstock first saw the Webb Brothers perform when they opened a show for their father at the Double Door in Chicago on October 23, 1998.

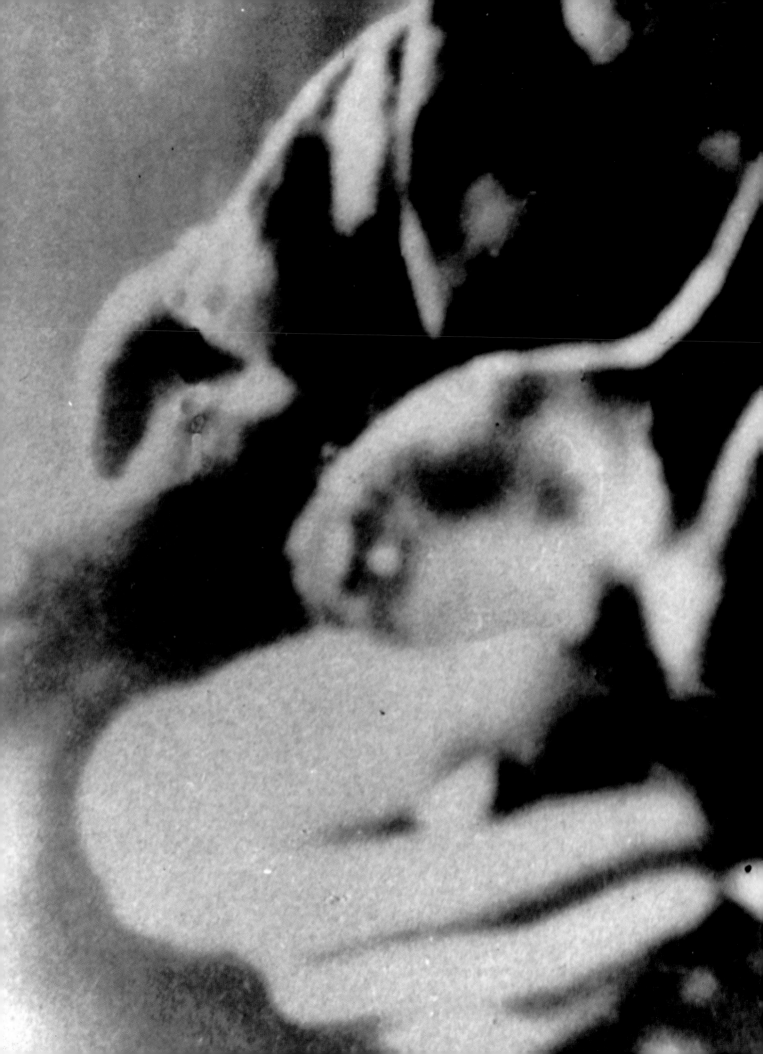

WILL THE FAMILY BE UNITED

For his descendants, Woody Guthrie's iconic legacy was intertwined with his harrowing illness. What has lasted, and bonded them, is his music.

by John Marks

On his fifth birthday, Arlo Guthrie got a guitar from his father, an itinerant and somewhat famous folk singer named Woody. Chaos — and a career — ensued.

Stories are the lifeblood of the Guthrie family, and a version of this one, as told by Arlo, goes like this: One day in Brooklyn — it was 1952 — Woody Guthrie set out from his home to buy a birthday present for his son. Sometimes when Woody left, he didn't come back for months at a time, but this trip wouldn't take so long. On his way out the door, a neighbor asked him where he was going, and Woody told him he was going to get a guitar for his kid. The neighbor asked him to buy one for his daughter as well.

Arlo's dad spent a fortune on the gifts — $70 each on a pair of three-quarter-size Gibsons.

The homecoming wasn't fun. "He came back, having spent $140 for two of these little guitars," recalls Arlo, "and the shit hit the fan. That's the only way to put it. Not only my mom, who was very economically conscious, but the neighbors were — livid is not the right word. They went ballistic. They didn't have any money. Nobody had any money where we were living. How could the neighbors be expected to pay back my dad for this guitar? Course he couldn't have cared less about being paid back. Money to him was nothing anyhow. He had to end up justifying it somehow, even if he didn't really care, so he said, 'Look, if you get the kid a toy, he'll play with it for two weeks, and that'll be the end of it. If you get him a real instrument, it will be a friend for life.'"

Arlo Guthrie

Arlo Guthrie is 62 years old now, his hair silver — that's how he describes the color anyway, according to his daughter Sarah Lee — but he still has the three-quarter-size Gibson, and so does the daughter of the Brooklyn neighbor. Her grandchildren now play it.

"My dad was a smart guy. In his own crazy way, he was absolutely right.

"You know what?" Guthrie reflected after telling me that story. We were sitting in a recording studio freshly built out of a converted barn in the woods outside Washington, Massachusetts. "My dad was a smart guy. In his own crazy way, he was absolutely right. He understood something that, to this day, most people don't get, and my mom would not have understood had the proof not been in the pudding."

He had a smile on his face when delivered the coda. "It was true for me. The guitar was a friend for life."

It's a great story, an elegantly simple account of the musical legacy passed from Woody Guthrie to his children and grandchildren, and yet it's not the whole story, which is more complicated and tragic than the one Arlo told. Another version appears in a book that Arlo's younger sister Nora recommended to me, Ed Cray's *Ramblin' Man*, an unfettered biographical account of the greatness and sickness of their father.

In that version, the historian writes, the guitar incident occurred shortly after Woody's 40th birthday, at the end of a protracted drama which began when the musician, despondent over his alcoholism and the damage it had done to his marriage and family, threatened to kill himself to his wife Marjorie, who telephoned the police. The police tracked the folk singer down to his Manhattan address, according to Cray, whereupon Guthrie voluntarily committed himself to Bellevue Hospital.

Shortly after his release from a monthlong stay at Bellevue, Cray goes on, Woody brought the guitars home, and here the two stories briefly converge. There was a fight over the instruments. In the midst of it, the singer hit his wife and one of the children.

Remorseful, according to Cray, Woody recommitted himself to the hospital, and, two months later, he was diagnosed with Huntington's Disease, the genetically inherited illness that had killed his mother and would eventually take his own life. From that time on, Huntington's Disease would become a decisive fact of life for his wife and children. They were witnesses to the physical disintegration of a man who had come to symbolize the most romantic and ambitious sentiments in American folk music, was a clear influence on his friends Pete Seeger and Ramblin' Jack Elliott, and be-

Above, and at right: Woody Guthrie at Cony Island, New York, with Arlo, Joady, and Nora. Photograph courtesy the Woody Guthrie Archives.

came an icon to a younger generation: Bob Dylan, Bruce Springsteen, Kris Kristofferson and Willie Nelson, among countless others.

Still, to his family, for many years, the legend of Woody Guthrie, American troubadour, paled beside the affliction of Huntington's.

Two poles of the Guthrie family legacy, then: the inspiration of the guitar and everything it meant and still means, and the sorrow of the illness and everything it came to mean. The legacy doesn't end there, by any stretch. But in a season when Arlo and his children — Abe, Cathy, Annie, and Sarah Lee and her husband Johnny Irion — are back on the road touring an economically and socially beleaguered America with Woody's songs, and when Nora Guthrie has been assisting Rounder Records in the release of new recordings of those songs and collaborating on a stunning photographic essay about her father's illness, the two things — music and illness — are increasingly inescapable.

Slowly but surely, through his family, a new version of the man is emerging.

I hear him, for instance, in Woody Guthrie's best-known song. Last spring, as I was getting to know members of the family and learning a bit more about the man himself, my fourth-grader came home and announced that his class would be studying Woody Guthrie in school. The year before, he told me, he'd learned "This Land Is Your Land," and I was struck by something.

As I thought about it, I couldn't recall if I had ever heard an original recording of that song. I could remember singing it myself in elementary school, and I remembered, in particular, hearing the song as if for the first time on Springsteen's album *Live/1975-1985*, but I couldn't actually recall a moment when I sat and listened to Woody Guthrie's version.

So I did, and it amazed me. On the face of it, despite its many fans, the song might be easily dismissed as either an over-familiar staple of campfire sing-alongs or an agitprop anthem of left-wing America. But the beauty of the song is that it's not an anthem, despite Springsteen's ringing and rather too strident rendition.

To my ears, listening to it as an adult with a greater knowledge of the man who wrote its lyrics, "This Land Is Your Land" strikes me as one of the most hauntingly and mournfully personal of all American folk songs, a poetic account of desperate consolation, one afflicted human being who finds himself only really at home in the wide, beautiful and terrifying spaces of the American landscape.

All discussion of those missing lines about "private property" aside, to hear Woody Guthrie sing, "I roamed and I rambled and I followed my footsteps to the sparkling sands of her diamond deserts" is not first and foremost to hear an argument about popular democracy; it's to hear the sound of a halting step in the back of your mind. It's to hear the love of country and the fear of sickness together, and to understand they may be inseparable in the man who wrote the lyric.

A few brief facts about Woody Guthrie: He was born on Bastille Day, 1912, in Okemah, Oklahoma, one of five siblings. Okemah became an oil boomtown for a few brief years, but is now best known as Guthrie's birthplace. The town fathers suppressed that fact for most of the last century because of Woody's politics, which were a mix of American populism, prairie Protestantism and loosely applied Communist principle. Free love figured big.

When Woody was 14, he heard his first harmonica, or so he always said. By the time he left Okemah three years later, he had his own, and played it on street corners and in bars. He was 17 when he left home. His eldest sister Clara was dead, killed in a mysterious accident

involving kerosene, a match and his mother. His father had narrowly escaped death in another incident of roughly the same kind. His mother had been committed to a hospital for the insane.

He ended up in Pampa, Texas, the first of many stops in a lifetime of travel around the country, a series of adventures that would become a seedbed for his songs. Inspired by acts such as the Carter Family and Bob Wills, encouraged by his friend Alan Lomax and accompanied often enough by Pete Seeger, Woody Guthrie wrote an estimated two to three thousand lyrics, only a few dozen of which were ever set to music.

By the time he was 40, he had been a cartoonist, a writer, a performer, and a political activist. He had married twice, once as a young man in Pampa, and a second time to a Jewish dancer named Marjorie Mazia. He had three children from his first marriage, and four from his second: Arlo (born in 1947), Joady (1948) and Nora (1950). Cathi, his first-born daughter with Marjorie, had been killed at age 4, a few months before Arlo was born, in one more fire-related calamity.

of his natural life, but it was just a chapter-break in the story of his music."

Woody's marriage to Marjorie eventually was strained by his wandering and his womanizing, and by the onset of Huntington's Disease. In 1967, at age 55, bedridden by his affliction and largely forgotten, he passed away, leaving behind yet a third wife and another child along with the wives and children from his first two marriages.

As is often the case in the biographies of great artists, his death marked the end of his natural life, but it was just a chapter-break in the story of his music — and the family members who would be influenced by it.

Sarah Lee Guthrie, Johnny Irion, and their daughter Olivia. Photograph by Michael Wilson.

Before I met Arlo, I went to visit his daughter Sarah Lee and her husband Johnny Irion, who have to be two of the busiest people in the music business. The couple have been married for a decade and singing together for almost as long, first on Irion's 2001 solo album *Unity Lodge* and eventually on their beguiling debut as a duo, 2005's *Exploration*.

When I met them at their home a few miles from Arlo's place in western Massachusetts, they'd just finished *Folksong*, a live album and accompanying DVD, and *Go Wagaloo*, a recording of infectious children's songs that incorporates the talents of several generations, from lyrics by grandfather Woody and accompaniment by his pal Pete Seeger to vocals courtesy of Johnny and Sarah Lee's 6-year-old daughter Olivia. A few weeks after that, in June, the couple went into the studio in Woodstock, New York, to record their follow-up to *Exploration*, assisted by members of the indie band Vetiver. This fall, they're on the road with father Arlo for the Guthrie Family Rides Again tour. (In August, Arlo released a historical live album titled *Tales Of '69* featuring three previously unrecorded songs.)

I asked Sarah Lee how she thought about her grandfather's legacy, especially in light of the upcoming tour and new records. She didn't talk much about sorrow. "It was inspiring," she told me flatly.

Yet, for years, she didn't know much at all about her famous grandfather.

"Arlo's not a pusher," Irion said, when I asked his wife that question. In another conversation, he told me with a certain amount of weariness that one thing it means to be Woody Guthrie's granddaughter is to be asked "the same goddamn question" again and again — i.e. what does it mean to be Woody Guthrie's granddaughter.

As a child, Sarah Lee and Arlo both told me, she hadn't been especially interested in music, much less her grandfather's, but she'd shown some promise as a singer. A rendition of David Mallett's "Garden Song" on her father's 1981 album *Power Of Love* features Sarah Lee — then a toddler — as part of a children's chorus backing up Arlo, along with her siblings Abe, Cathy and Annie plus a few family friends (including, interestingly, future Beck and R.E.M. drummer Joey Waronker).

When Sarah Lee was 14, her father asked her to sing along with Pete Seeger on Seeger's song "Sailing Down My Golden River" for a concert at Wolf Trap, a sizable venue near Washington, D.C. "I wasn't scared," she said. "I don't know why. Maybe I should have been, but I wasn't. I kind of felt confident that Dad had asked me to do it, so I must be able to do it. He saw something in me that maybe I didn't. I was sort of handed the torch at that point, and I took it pretty seriously, because Dad never let us on-stage. It was a very deliberate hand-off."

"Just for the hell of it," Arlo told me later with visible pride, "I had the three girls up on-stage, singing, and with absolute fearlessness, although she was shaking, Sarah got up there and sang 'Sailing Down My Golden River' in front of 20,000 people. Never sang a thing in her life, but sang it in tune and just bulldogged her way through it, just looked it in the eye and went and did it."

Sarah Lee Guthrie and Johnny Irion rehearsing. Photograph by Michael Traister.

After that, Sarah Lee Guthrie told me, she became a "crazy teenager," and the adventure in folk music came to a temporary end. She shaved her head and became a punk, outraging her parents and giving her father a lot of that silver hair. As a result, she served out the bulk of her teenage years on an ashram in Florida. It wasn't until she moved to California and met Johnny Irion that her musical gene kicked back in and she discovered her grandfather.

Guthrie and Irion have built a life together on music. They live in a two-story A-Frame cabin on a hundred acres of western Massachusetts land, and they write and even record songs within its walls. Both are lanky and good-looking. He's got a trim beard, and she has long brunette hair. Onstage, their voices complement, and on the page, so do their lyrics, though they have very different writing styles. She has an easy way with words and dashes off her lines in a notebook. She doesn't like to formalize the process. He's an agonizer and favors bearing down hard in the process.

They have two daughters, Olivia and Sophie, who are surrounded by aunts and uncles and cousins. Guthrie and Irion live in the vicinity of most of her family, the progeny of Woody and Marjorie of Brooklyn. Their cabin in the hills is a long way from Coney Island; it's a folkie dream, with boards of redwood, white oak and cherry, warm in the long New England winters, cool in the summers, though the couple are on the road for much of the year and don't always get to enjoy its pleasures as much as they would like. These days, they call themselves folk singers, but it wasn't always that way.

In the beginning, they shunned the label. When they were formally introduced in a bar in West Hollywood, she was still into punk bands such as Minor Threat, and he had just come under the spell of California country, an urban redneck cocktail that included plenty of Gram Parsons, Buffalo Springfield, and Merle Haggard. Listening to their record *Exploration*, on songs like "Cease Fire" and "In Lieu Of Flowers," they sound a lot more like George Jones and Tammy Wynette than the Weavers.

The impression becomes even more pronounced when they tell the story of their initial courtship on the canyon roads of Los Angeles. At times, as I turned back and forth between them, listening, I had the feeling I was in an early 1960s Nashville duet, something Johnny and June might have sung.

A mutual friend introduced them at a bar where a bluegrass band played. "After that, I called several times," Irion told me. "She would not call me back."

"I was only 18," she said.

"She was very shy," he said. "She won't talk on the phone."

"He talked me into coming to pick him up one night," she said, "and I did."

"No," he corrected. "You said I'll pick you up, and I said fine."

"Actually," she continued, "I gave you the wrong phone number, and you gave me the wrong address, and I was just driving around the neighborhood, and I see this guy walking down the street in a cowboy hat, and I thought that must be him."

They went to a bar, where the underaged Guthrie used her sister's ID to get in. At that point in our interview, she said — more to Irion than to me — she was ready to call the whole thing off. "I asked you, 'How old are you anyway?' and you said, 'I'm 28,' and I said, 'We should go. You're way too old for me.'"

He begged to differ. "I think I said, 'We should go. You're way too young for me.'"

"Either way," concluded Guthrie, "we agreed on one more drink, and that was pretty much it. We were inseparable after that."

Moving in together meant, among other things, making music together. They shared an apartment with a drummer and a steel guitar player; everyone had day jobs. Irion and a pal, Mike Stinson, were playing gigs, but whenever possible, from the end of the work day until dawn, the housemates made their way through the songs of the Louvin Brothers, Little Feat, Buffalo Springfield, and the collected works of Gram Parsons. Guthrie got a job at a record store and started to bring albums home. Irion taught her to pick out a few songs on guitar. They both discovered Gillian Welch, and her record *Revival* shot one more spark into the mix.

Guthrie began to explore her own musical roots, and the first stop was her father Arlo. "I came home for Christmas," she said, "and I raided the record collection. I also got a guitar.

I found a 1920s LG Gibson in a closet. I found it all dusty with a bunch of other guitars, and I thought, this one suits me just fine. It was small and had a great sound. I didn't even ask. I just took the kit back to L.A. I thought, no one's going to miss this. And I opened it up. I said, 'Johnny, check out what I got.'"

Like father, like daughter. One thing led to another, and finding the old guitar led to her grandfather, who until that time was little more than a remote presence in her life. "I didn't know anything about Woody Guthrie," she confessed. "I just didn't. I knew my dad's songs. I was sort of put into the fire a few times to learn 'This Land Is Your Land' and that kind of stuff, but that was it. I didn't know anything that I do now about his life. I never read the book. I didn't look at the movie."

Later, Arlo offered his philosophy about passing his father's legacy onto his kids. "I don't think I did much at all," he said. "I just let them grow up. At some point or other, they, like me, discovered people singing 'This Land Is Your Land.' I did not sit them down and teach them the words or even warn them this might happen, but at some point, each one, in a different way, was trying to get a little closer to that fire."

With his son Abe, it started at age 3. "Abe had a Big Wheel — he traded it for a keyboard to a kid on the street," Arlo recalled. "At 3 years old, you don't know what a grandfather is, let alone one that's famous, but he knew he wanted to play music, and he's been doing it ever since."

Arlo Guthrie as an instrument of change, in a 1970s Reprise promotional photo.

"And I remember Cathy, my oldest daughter," he went on, "after a couple of semesters of college, called me up and said, 'Look, Pop, don't get upset, it's just a ukulele, it's only got four strings, it's not like a guitar.' I said, 'It starts with four.' She called me about six months later and said, 'Pop, can you get me a banjo?' I said, 'See? Five. Next thing you'll want a guitar.' Sure enough she did. By that time, it was too late." (Cathy eventually teamed up with Willie Nelson's daughter Amy in a duo called Folk Uke.)

Annie, who her father says "couldn't carry a tune," now sings and writes her own songs. And then there was Sarah.

After leaving the ashram, she managed Arlo on tour, but hadn't shown the slightest interest in following in his footsteps as a musician. When she met Irion, everything changed. "She brought a guitar home one day and said, 'Pop, show me how to play it.' I said sure, right, I'll show her a couple of chords. I showed her the chords, and about three days later, she came back, and her fingers were bleeding, there was blood on the guitar neck, and that's when I knew she was going to do it."

He took her on the road and taught her what he knew. Within a few years, he said, she was onstage and stealing his routines.

to get a little closer to that fire." — Arlo Guthrie

Meanwhile, her fascination with her grandfather grew, but her dad wasn't the real authority on the subject. For that, she turned to her Aunt Nora, the custodian of the Woody Guthrie Foundation and Archives, the person who has arguably done more than anyone else to revive and transform the meaning of Woody Guthrie's legacy in the popular culture.

Arlo and Nora and their brother Joady share the same mother and father, but, as Arlo and Nora both made clear to me, their memories of childhood differ in significant ways. "A year or two can make an awful big difference when you're that young," Arlo told me. "My mom was married a number of times after that. But my father was daddy to me, and not to my brother and sister in the same way, because of that year difference between me and my brother, and two-and-a-half-year difference between me and my sister. I never bought into the fatherness of the stepdads, and my siblings tried to adjust as best they could in that way."

Arlo was just old enough, in other words, to know the man who was not wholly consumed by Huntington's Disease. "I always retained enough memories of my dad for him to be daddy to me," he said. "And most of those memories are back when I'm 2 or 3 or 4 years old, and they're just fleeting glimpses of things — the sound of his voice, the feeling of his presence, and those kinds of things that are, unless I volunteered to go under some hypnotic therapy, I couldn't make a whole lot of sense of them. I remember the smells and the tastes of the times; they come back every once in a while in the strangest moments."

For Nora, the moments that linger are dominated by disease. Every Sunday, without fail, she and her family would go to the ward of a mental hospital, most memorably Ward 40 at Greystone Hospital in New Jersey, or her father would return home from the ward for the day, to be fed chocolate cake and whole milk to keep up his calorie intake. "We experienced my dad sick most of the time," she told me. "It's not like he walked into a room and the flashlights were on him. We all took care of him for fifteen years, and taking care of a Huntington's patient is tough. It's not a pretty disease. It's an ugly disease. It's a messy disease."

The memory lies especially close to the surface at the moment, perhaps, because Nora has been working with photographer Philip Buehler and Abrams Books to publish a harrowing photographic and written document of her father's years at Greystone. Titled *Wardy Forty*, which was Woody Guthrie's sardonic name for the place where he spent seven years of his life, the book consists of a series of photographs taken by Buehler on the 1,000-acre grounds of a hospital that was once the largest in the United States.

Greystone Hospital has a special significance in the annals of folk music, because it was here, in 1961, that Bob Dylan paid a visit to his hero, Woody Guthrie, ultimately penning "Song To Woody" in the aftermath of the encounter. Other pilgrims and fellow travelers made their way to pay tribute, among them Ramblin' Jack Elliott and Pete Seeger, and the book chronicles those moments in photographs, but the truly haunting stuff is the documentation of the abandonment of the hospital.

When Buehler visited, he didn't just find the hospital in ruins. He found files and papers scattered across the floor, including photographs taken of Woody Guthrie when he was admitted. In Buehler's photos, Greystone is a spectral wreck, a Pentagon-sized mass of stone and ghost, like one of those Soviet military bases abandoned by the Russian army at the end of the Cold War — walls peeling with old paint, typewriters left standing, metal beds placed in a row.

Arlo went out to have a look and gather up whatever other papers he could find. Nora declined. It was too much for her. She had vivid memories of Greystone as a child, including a tree dubbed by her father the Magickry Tree, where she and her siblings used to play. She didn't need to go back. The Magickry Tree was there in the photographs, too, still standing. Her way of grappling with the tree — and the past — wasn't to go back. Rather, it was to work with Buehler on the book, which is due out in the spring of 2010.

"Most people have the first twenty years of their parents," Nora said, "playing ball and family vacations, and then their parents get old and get sick, and they end up taking care of them. The sad story comes after the good story. In our family life, it was exactly the opposite. The sad story was in the beginning. For me, personally, it wasn't until I worked in the archives and I created it, that I saw the songs about

The Magickry Tree, then (with Woody, Marjorie, and Nora, 1960, courtesy Nora Guthrie) and now, a juxtaposition from photographer Phillip Buehler's forthcoming book, Wardy Forty.

baseball and the fun and Walt Whitman's niece, all this material that made me smile. Everyone should smile when they think of Woody, but that was the first time I smiled when I thought of Woody."

These days, Nora spends a lot of her time smiling. In a very real sense, the Woody Guthrie Foundation and Archives has given her a shot at a second childhood with her father.

In addition to a new relationship with Rounder Records, which recently released a box set of Woody Guthrie standards taken from newly discovered master recordings called *My Dusty Road*, she's also been working with Jay Farrar on a few of her father's songs, and spreading the word far and wide that he was more than just a dust bowl balladeer. As if she needed proof, she points to the wild and unexpected success of "Shipping Up To Boston," the unofficial punk anthem of the Boston Red Sox victory in the World Series — lyrics by her father, music by the Dropkick Murphys.

It's the biggest hit yet in the archive's ongoing effort to put Woody Guthrie's bank of un-recorded lyrics into the hands of contemporary artists, and nothing could please her more than such an out-of-left-field triumph. Knocking folkie heads has been a favorite pastime ever since the 1998 success of the collaboration between Billy Bragg and Wilco on *Mermaid Avenue*, the moment when the heirs of Woody Guthrie let the folk music world know that the paterfamilias was really a big old punk rocker in sheep's clothing.

I met Nora at the Woody Guthrie Foundation and Archives in midtown Manhattan, a small suite of rooms down a labyrinthine hall in a high-rise office building on West 57th Street. It's an unlikely place to find her father's life's work, a surprising range of material that in-cludes, in addition to almost 3,000 separate lyrics (most of which have never been set to music), an assortment of poetry, drawings, novels, essays and more. While there, I listened to a German version of a song called "Neunzig Meilen Orkan" or "Ninety Mile Storm," recorded by a Berlin artist named Hans-Eckart Wenzel. The sound steeps a hint of Americana in a musical beer stein of Kurt Weill and Bertolt Brecht, and the result is striking. It's Woody as cabaret, and it works.

The record, called *Ticky Tock*, was released in English and German versions in 2003, and Nora loved the sound so much, she booked Wenzel into a "Nashville Sings Woody" show at the Ry-man Auditorium. The audience response was underwhelming, but that came as no surprise.

"Some people loved it," she told me. "Some people hated it. People who are into the folk thing said it wasn't Woody, but how can you say that a guy steeped in Brecht and Weill isn't Woody. It's the same musical family, they just speak a different language, and they have a dif-ferent style of presentation. Weill is the Woody Guthrie of Germany, as far as I can tell, but I'm a little mischievous that way."

Ever since she opened the archives in 1996 with the help of curator Jorge Arrevalo, she has relished the opportunity to smash the graven image of her father held up by the old-line folk fans: The lightly dusted Woody, always in sepia tone, just as he appears in the iconic pho-tograph with the guitar that reads, "This Machine Kills Fascists." Nora has nothing against that image, but she rebels against the idea that it's the sole lens through which to see her father.

When I asked her about the impact of someone like Dylan on her father's image, she credited Dylan with rescuing her father from obscurity in the 1960s. "I love him," she said. "I have not one negative thing to say about him. He served such a calling. At the right time in the right place, when Woody first passed away, when he was in his last days, Bob Dylan held the bridge, which would have broken if it hadn't been for him and Jack Elliott. I see one of these walking bridges in a Tibetan rain forest, or something, and certain people came along at a certain time and held it together because there was no organization, there was no archives, there were a few thousand people who knew or cared, and he took it upon himself, consciously or unconsciously. Woody was dying at one end, and there was the future at the other end, so Dylan was that little walking bridge hanging five thousand feet above the river. As far as I'm concerned, he's done his life's work for me. I don't ask him for anything, expect anything from him. He's done what he came here to do for my father, and no one could have done it more brilliantly than he did, and I'm eternally grateful."

At the same time, when she talks about the future of her father's music, she's more likely to bring up the Clash. "People say Bob Dylan, and I say Joe Strummer," she says. "My father's music changed Joe Strummer's life. There's a whole long legacy of Woody in punk."

In Nora's presence, listening to her talk about how she sees the future of her father's music, its connection to other languages and peoples, to future generations, it's easy to imagine a time when the clichéd image of Woody Guthrie in the 20th century dwindles to insignificance. Legacies are funny things. They can seem so fixed, and yet over time they morph and change, just like the natural landscape. The greater the legacy, one could argue, the more universal its scope, the greater the likelihood of transformation over time.

This fall, however, as the other heirs to the tradition travel around the United States singing his songs and a few of their own, something tells me it's the old, familiar Woody of the Great Depression that will be most relevant. If there has ever been a time since the era when he first started singing and writing songs when Woody Guthrie's vision of America had more resonance, I can't think of it. The '60s appreciated him, but that was an era of prosperity. The translation was indirect. Arlo and Sarah Lee and company will be touring in a land where millions have lost their jobs in a matter of months, where homes are being foreclosed, businesses are shutting down, families are disintegrating, and tempers are rising. "I Ain't Got No Home" will be no one's idea of nostalgia.

Touring family (l. to r.): Sarah Lee, Arlo, and Abe Guthrie, and Johnny Irion. Photograph by Bryan Rierson.

The way Arlo sees it, most people still fail to understand his father, what he actually stood for as opposed to what he seems to represent. At the core is neither universal brotherhood nor folk music. Something else informs the sensibility.

"I've read all of the books that people have written about him," Arlo told me, "but I don't think anybody's really caught his spirit quite yet. They don't understand the feeling of what he was personally striving to do. He was a driven guy. What really drove him — above all the other little drives — the big one was the desire to be free. He really didn't want to have to explain himself to himself or to the Divine or to anything in between, and he succeeded. He had learnt to be detached, and he practiced it on purpose."

"He wouldn't sleep in beds, I remember. He didn't want to get soft. He wanted to be able to get up and go at a moment's notice, so he didn't want things, and people tried to give him things. They gave him cars, they gave him guitars, they gave him money, they gave him clothing, shoes, whatever you think a person would need, and he abandoned it all. They gave him relationships. He abandoned it all, not because he was crazy, not be cause he was sick, but because he was purposefully intent on practicing the disciplines that would allow him to be free, with no strings, no expectations, no judgment, and he actually succeeded.

"I think that's part of why his legacy is so strong, because this underlying hint of freedom is what attracts; it's like moths to the flame, so you get the Dylans and the Phil Ochs, and the other characters who have come by over the years. It's not the songs, it's not the writing; that's all part of it, but there's more to it than that, there's something underlying it. They want to know how he got there. How does a person write these songs? How does a person see the world the way he sees it? The only glimpse you get is that the price you have to pay for that is too high. So people back off and end up being themselves."

Finally, that's the thing Arlo Guthrie, the man and the musician, most admires about his father, and maybe the most profound thing he's passed on about his father to his children. "Most people can't pay the price," he said. "They can't afford it. To me, I admire that most about him. The very thing most people disparage about him is the thing I absolutely adore about him. I mean I'm not a son, I'm a disciple. I get it. I'm so happy to be in the presence of somebody like that. It's not about being related. That's the smallest part of it."

Before I left his home, Arlo offered one more memory. Shortly after his dad got him that three-quarter-size Gibson guitar, he took it to a luncheonette, where he sat at the counter and began to strum. At 5 years old, he couldn't play the thing to save his life, and one of the patrons shooed him out the door. He came across an empty lot near the luncheonette and in embarrassment hid the guitar in some weeds.

When he came home without it, he told me, his mother became furious. "She read me the riot act."

But the storm passed, and they found the guitar. The rest, as they say, is Guthrie family history.

John Marks is the author most recently of the memoir Reasons To Believe: One Man's Journey Among The Evangelicals And The Faith He Left Behind *and the novel* Fangland. *He blogs at www.purplestateofmind.com. His mother's parents are from Checotah, Oklahoma, just down Interstate 40 from Okemah, birthplace of Woody Guthrie.*

Of time and rivers flowing

The long and tangled roots of the Seegers
run throughout modern American folk music

by JESSE FOX MAYSHARK

IN THE SPRING OF 1939, the March-April edition of the learned journal *Modern Music* opened with a challenge to its high-minded, harmonically sophisticated readers: to open up their cultured, discriminating ears to the songs of the nation around them, "an art totally unknown, or unrecognized, by the bulk of the American professional musicians."

For decades, the essay argued, American composers and musical scholars had yearned for and tried to summon into being a truly native music, one that would transcend the overbearing influences of European stylists and Old World aesthetics. "The first break in this jam came, I think," the essayist wrote, "in 1925 and '26 with the realization that the jazz boys had hit upon something the academic or fine-art composer had missed." But the jazz boys were just the latest page in the story; the reality was that while generations of aspiring American musicians had been dutifully absorbing the latest innovations and theories on the Continent, the people of their own country had been building and refining a rapidly growing and mutating body of homespun musical art that had escaped the notice of the urban academies the same way wheatfields es-

cape the notice of butterfly collectors. It was taken for granted as part of the land-scape. But the landscape, the essayist insisted, was what mattered. The essay was titled "Grass Roots for American Composers." Its author was a prominent, if ec-centric and fiercely opinion-ated, musical scholar named Charles Louis Seeger.

"[G]ather together a dozen average people from various parts of the country," he admonished his reader-ship, "people who are not too ingrained with the prejudic-es of music-professionalism, great wealth or smartness, add a guitar or a banjo (no piano), and see how many songs you can get out of them — 'folk-songs' if you're

Professor Charles Louis Seeger, violinist Constance de Clyver Edson and family, March 23, 1921. Image courtesy the National Photo Company Collection, Library of Congress Prints and Photographs Division.

a sophisticate, 'old songs' or mere 'songs' if you are nice and common. Will there not be 'Down In The Valley' and 'Careless Love'? And how about 'Frankie And Johnnie,' 'Wreck Of The Old Ninety-Seven,' 'Red River Valley,' 'John Henry,' 'Shortnin' Bread,' 'Cripple Creek,' 'Maple On

The Hill,' 'Buffalo Gals,' 'Barbara Allen'? Perhaps there will be 'Jesse James,' 'Sam Bass,' 'Old Joe Clark,' or even 'The Golden Vanity,' 'Pretty Saro,' 'Lord Lovel.'

"How long would the list be before the possibilities of even a casual gathering could be exhausted?" Seeger asked. "Really I do not know and doubt if anyone does." He mentioned "blind old Mrs. Dusenberry in Arkansas," who knew 113 songs, and Bascom Lamar Lunsford in North Carolina, who could sing 315. "No matter how elaborate the survey of the actual music made by the people of America upon the basis of a purely oral tradition, it is to be doubted we could ever plumb the bottom of this deep well-spring."

"If I Had An Axe?" Peter Seeger, May 23, 1921. Image courtesy the National Photo Company Collection, Library of Congress Prints and Photographs Division.

The essay was an academic's cry of aspirational populism, and it mirrored its author's own evolution from ivory-tower theorist to activist and advocate. Seventy years later, it also reads like a primer for what has become a sprawling family project. It began with Charles and was amplified by his second wife, Ruth Crawford Seeger, and has carried on through children, grandchildren and great-grandchildren, spreading across cultures and continents, bumping up often against history (and less often, but maybe more than you'd think, against the pop charts), and asserting at every step something Charles Seeger wrote in that essay: "A music has its life in the making of it. It is not the music they listen to that is the music of a people, but the music people make for themselves."

The best-known bearer of the Seeger name is Pete, the youngest son from Charles Seeger's first marriage. For his music and his activism, which have never really been separate, he is revered as something like a saint in some liberal and artistic quarters. (In May, those quarters included Madison Square Garden, where Pete Seeger's 90th birthday was feted with a four-hour benefit concert that included appearances by Bruce Springsteen, Kris Kristofferson, Emmylou Harris, Joan Baez, John Mellencamp, Arlo Guthrie, and a score of others.) But Pete's work makes most sense seen within the context of his family. From Charles and Ruth onward, there has been a sort of entwined mission of preservation and performance, scholarship and activism. In the hands of the Seegers, music is a vehicle both for conserving the past and agitating for the future. Different members of the family have taken up different aspects of that work, and of course not all of them are directly engaged in it at all.

"There's actually about 110 of us," says Peggy Seeger, Pete's younger half-sister and the second child of Charles and Ruth, "and I would say probably twenty of us are in music. But the others have a great tolerance for folk music, I will tell you, although there's one or two that have gone into more popular music."

The through-line of the Seegers' work is sometimes literal: Pete, Peggy, and Peggy's brother Mike recorded songs they learned from their parents, often for albums on the Folkways label that were then reissued decades later by their nephew Anthony, a musicologist who oversaw the label's catalogue after it was purchased by the Smithsonian. Some of those songs also appear in more modern settings on records by the Mammals, the folk-rock band co-founded earlier this decade by Pete's grandson Tao Rodriguez-Seeger.

But the family's influence extends far beyond its own bounds. The work that Charles and Ruth Seeger started was in some ways utopian — they thought that teaching American songs to Americans could help forge a new sense of shared national identity. But it was also clear-eyed and unflinching. How could it be otherwise, given the nature of the songs they were championing as the people's music? "John Henry," "Frankie And Johnny," "Wreck Of The Old 97" — songs about struggle and dehumanization, betrayed love, the persistent nearness of death, which sat comfortably alongside joke songs and romantic ballads and tall tales. The music demands a certain honesty about the pains and sorrows of life, without precluding its capacity for joy. And, crucially, that joy is embodied, or at least represented, in the act of making music itself.

Mike and Peggy Seeger, 1955. Photograph courtesy Peggy Seeger.

David King Dunaway, who wrote the definitive biography *How Can I Keep From Singing: The Ballad Of Pete Seeger*, said in an interview that the Seegers' ideas about the transformative power of song — the potential of music to unite people in common purpose — cannot be separated from the ferment of the Depression and the rise of Popular Front leftism in the 1930s, when Pete was a teenager and Charles was making his shift toward folk music.

"There is an obvious and important parallel between the moment in historical time when the Left sings in harmony with Roosevelt and the time when Pete Seeger grows up as an adolescent and begins singing with people," Dunaway says.

And so when Bruce Springsteen, at the 90th birthday concert, called Pete Seeger "a stealth dagger through the heart of our country's illusions about itself," it was only half the story. Pete's work, like much of his family's, has been not only about exposing the nation's failure to live up to its assorted mythologies of freedom and justice. It has also been about trying to make those mythologies real — trying to bring harmony from discord.

"He absolutely fits into a paradigm of American independence," Dunaway says of Pete Seeger, "of a freethinking — and that's the word that was used — a freethinking Puritan tradition. And that goes back to the founding of our nation."

THE SEEGERS GO BACK to the founding of the nation, too, and beyond. For all their populism, they have an impeccable American pedigree. They claim Mayflower lineage, and ancestors fought against the British in the Revolutionary War, and for the union in the Civil War. The family's 20th-century turn toward radicalism might seem like a break from that line; Charles Seeger, then 30, was essentially hounded out of his first job, as a professor at the University of California, after he registered as a conscientious objector to World War I. In his 20s, he had developed increasingly radical politics, first through exposure to the lives and working conditions of California migrant workers, and then to the ideas of Industrial Workers of the World, which was organizing them.

At the same time, his brother, Alan — like Charles, a Harvard graduate — was so eager to join what he saw as a noble cause that he enlisted in the French Foreign Legion before the United States even entered the war. He was killed in battle on the Fourth of July in 1916, and family pride in his service has been handed down side-by-side with pride in Charles' principled refusal to serve. Pete Seeger — who served in World War II after initially opposing it, and has been an anti-war activist ever since — has often publicly recited Alan's battlefield poem "Rendezvous With Death," which Alan wrote about six months before he died. It seems like a contradictory legacy, but it illuminates something central to the family's credo: a willingness to stand up for ideals, and to suffer for them. Alan lost his life, and Charles lost his job, both of them in service to something they believed. That those beliefs put them on opposite sides of the same issue is in some ways less important.

Pete Seeger entertaining Eleanor Roosevelt, honored guest at an integrated 1944 Valentine's Day party to mark the opening of the United Federal Labor Canteen in Washington, D.C.. Photograph by Joseph Horne for the Office of War Information, courtesy Library of Congress Prints and Photographs Division.

There are, really, many contradictions in the family's narrative threads. Political liberals, and sometimes radicals, they have also often been strikingly conservative in their approach to culture and lifestyle. Although Pete Seeger was a sort of accidental godfather of folk-rock, thanks to the Byrds' recording of "Turn! Turn! Turn!," he never developed much of a taste for rock 'n' roll. Mike Seeger has made a career of recording largely pre-World War II songs and styles of folk music, both as a performer and a producer. Peggy has written hundreds of songs, as did her husband of three decades, the influential British ballad singer Ewan MacColl, but mostly within traditional forms. At times they seem arrayed against both the reactionary and the modern.

"Most of my family don't even have computers," says Tao Rodriguez-Seeger, the son of Pete's daughter Mika. "My mother still doesn't know how to answer her e-mail. It's funny that we're such a, you might call it, revolutionary-progressive family, yet at the same time riddled with Luddites."

THAT TENSION FIRST surfaced in the musical trajectories of Charles and Ruth Seeger, who both started out as determined modernists. Charles was a pioneer in the field of musicology, the study of how music functions formally, historically and culturally, but much of his early work was in theoretical realms. It was his work on dissonant counterpoint that first attracted Ruth Crawford to him. They met in 1929, when she moved to New York from Chicago, where she had established a reputation as a talented young composer. She was also a close family friend of Carl Sandburg, who had written her a letter of recommendation for a Guggenheim Fellowship.

At 28 and unmarried, Ruth Crawford was part of a generation of well-educated women determined to redefine the social parameters of acceptable female ambition. As Judith Tick records in her invaluable biography *Ruth Crawford Seeger: A Composer's Search For American Music*, that meant putting up with responses like the one from the critic who said admiringly that her preludes were "anything but feminine." But it also meant she was able to pursue a real artistic career. Charles was fifteen years her senior, and their relationship

Charles Louis Seeger, Peggy Seeger (age 2), and Ruth Crawford Seeger. Photograph courtesy Peggy Seeger.

began as mentor-student. But over a few years, it matured into an intellectual partnership, and then into a romance. (Charles' marriage to Pete's mother, a classical violinist named Constance de Clyver Edson, had started to fray several years before.)

"They were a good match," Peggy Seeger says of Ruth and Charles. "They followed the usual pattern in that you marry your opposite. My father was tall, stringy, gentle, rarely lost his temper. He wasn't as creative as my mother. My mother was short, stocky, a peasant build — though I hesitate to use that. She was fiery, had a temper. She played the piano absolutely wonderfully, with fire. My father played gently. He chose the more gentle Chopin/Dvorak pieces, and my mother chose the ones where you whack the piano."

They married in 1932, and their first child was born the next August. Tick's biography quotes a letter from Ruth in the hospital to her husband: "Baby Michael is such a delicious little mystery…the dearest little piece of you." Peggy was born two years later, followed by two younger sisters, Barbara and Penny.

At first, the Seegers lived in New York, where they were part of a churning cultural and political scene. They were both active in a branch of the Workers Music League, which had as its slogan, "Music as a Weapon in the Class Struggle." Pete, by then a teenager, visited home from boarding school, and absorbed his father and stepmother's politics. He also absorbed their growing interest in music to match their proletarian instincts. Ruth and Charles were regulars at Saturday

The Seegers, at home in Washington, D.C., roughly 1937 (l. to r.): Ruth Crawford Seeger, Mike Seeger, Charles Louis Seeger, and Peggy Seeger. Photograph courtesy Mike Seeger.

night parties in the Greenwich Village apartment of the painter Thomas Hart Benton and his wife (Benton and Charles Seeger both taught at the New School for Social Research). Benton would play folk songs, sometimes accompanied by his art students, including a young Jackson Pollock. At one of these parties, a tagalong Pete Seeger first heard the song "John Henry."

But they lived on little money, and were close to homeless several times. So a job offer from one of President Roosevelt's New Deal agencies in 1935 was accepted with enthusiasm. Charles went to work for the Resettlement Administration, training musicians to work in communities of people displaced by the Depression. The family moved to Maryland. In 1937, Ruth was invited by the folklorist and song collector John Lomax to write transcriptions of his field recordings for an anthology of American folk songs under the auspices of the Library of Congress. She worked closely with Lomax's son, Alan, and her immersion in the songs, combined with Charles' enthusiasm for what he had come to think of as the nation's indigenous music, inevitably carried over to the household.

"She worked at home," says Peggy, who is 74, "and we'd play in the corner while she transcribed these weird people singing — people that now, I remember that I heard the real gems. I heard the originals. And then at night, when my father came home, they had dinner, and we were in bed, she'd sit down and play classical music at the piano for an hour or two. It was an incredible education, those two things put together."

Ruth eventually extended at least part of that education to the nation at large. In the 1940s, while working with music programs at schools in the Washington, D.C., area, she decided to compile some of the transcriptions she had done for the Lomaxes into a book for younger audiences. *American Folk Songs For Children* was published in 1948, just five years before Ruth died of cancer, and helped introduce songs such as "She'll Be Coming Round The Mountain When She Comes" and "Frog Went A-Courtin'" into the grade-school repertoire. It was followed by others, including *Animal Folk Songs For Children* and *American Folk Songs For Christmas*. All were popular, and if they took her far from her original ambitions as a composer, they reflected the convictions about music as a cultural force that she and Charles shared. In the introduction to the first children's collection, she wrote that the music it contained "bears many fingermarks. It has been handled roughly and gently. It has been used…It is not 'finished' or crystallized — it invites improvisation and creative aliveness….It invites participation."

OF COURSE, INVITING participation in certain kinds of activities was what repeatedly brought the Seegers to the attention of assorted authorities over the years. Pete, who dropped out of Harvard in the late 1930s, distilled his father's cerebral populism into a sort of sunny, communitarian radicalism. He briefly worked for Alan Lomax at the Library of Congress, while immersing himself in folk music and learning to play the banjo. Hungry for experience, musical and otherwise, he befriended Woody Guthrie at a benefit concert and ended up touring the country with him. And he became increasingly active in the labor movement and the Communist Party. The people he wanted to lead in song were people at rallies and Party conventions. He was dedicated enough to the Communist line that he and his first folk group, the Almanac Singers, initially took a hard stance against American involvement in World War II. (Hitler's pact with Stalin had the effect in the United States of making both the isolationist right and the Daily Worker left suspicious of Roosevelt's interventionism.)

Pete changed his tune after Pearl Harbor, literally: In 1942, he wrote a song called "Dear Mr. President" in which he promised to "Quit playing this banjo around with the boys/ And exchange it for something that makes more noise." He was drafted into the Army, but he took his banjo with him. Both Stateside and in the South Pacific, where he coordinated entertainment for wounded soldiers at a hospital on Saipan, he kept playing music. A photo

Playing the chords of change: Peggy Seeger (below left) onstage in Moscow, 1957, photograph courtesy Peggy Seeger; the Weavers (l. to r.) Pete Seeger, Lee Hays, Fred Hellerman, and Ronnie Gilbert.

in Dunaway's book shows him strumming and singing for a group of sailors and Eleanor Roosevelt.

But after the war, Pete quickly gravitated again to leftist and labor causes. He and his friend Lee Hays, who had been in the Almanac Singers, formed an organization called People's Songs. The goal, Seeger told Dunaway, was to form "a singing labor movement." He envisioned "hundreds, thousands, tens of thousands of union choruses. Just as every church has a choir, why not every union?" As it turned out, People's Songs garnered less attention from an increasingly pragmatic and anti-communist labor movement than it did from the Red-hunting FBI. As Pete sang on picket lines and campaigned for the 1948 presidential bid of Progressive Party candidate Henry Wallace, he was often under the eye of J. Edgar Hoover's agents. The attention lingered when Seeger and Hays formed the Weavers with two younger singers, Ronnie Gilbert and Fred Hellerman. Although their songs were less overtly radical than those of the Almanacs, they had a political sensibility that was made clear in their first record, released at the end of 1949. It was a song Seeger and Hays wrote together, called "If I Had A Hammer."

The next year, the Weavers surprised everyone, including themselves, with a huge commercial hit. Their recording of "Good Night Irene," which Pete had learned from Lead Belly (Alan Lomax had introduced them in 1939), went to #1. Without Lead Belly's verse about taking morphine, it was innocuous enough that Frank Sinatra promptly recorded his own hit version. But the heightened profile just ratcheted up official scrutiny of the band and its members' past associations.

They weren't actually called to testify by the House Un-American Activities Committee until August 1955, a year after Senator Joseph McCarthy had been censured in the Senate and the Red Scare had started to lose some steam. But HUAC operated on its own track, and blacklists were still in effect throughout the entertainment industry (even if they were largely unacknowledged).

Hays testified the day before Seeger did, and like many witnesses cited the Fifth Amendment in his refusal to answer questions about his political views or party affiliations. Taking the Fifth was generally enough to satisfy the symbolic goals of the hearings, since it implied a certain amount of acknowledged guilt. The panel was less interested in investigating its witnesses than humiliating them. But Seeger was not willing to accommodate either aim. When he was called to testify, instead of the Fifth Amendment, he cited the First.

Directly addressing the chairman, Representative Francis Walter of Pennsylvania, Seeger said: "I am not going to answer any questions as to my association, my philosophical or religious beliefs or my political beliefs, or how I voted in any election or any of these private affairs. I think these are very improper questions for any American to be asked, especially under such compulsion as this."

Pete Seeger at a peace rally, New York City, 1965. Photograph by Diana Davies.

When further questioning yielded nothing, the committee warned Seeger that he would face a charge of contempt of Congress. The charge did eventually come, although not until 1961. Seeger was found guilty in a New York federal court, but both the indictment and conviction were thrown out on appeal the next year. Still, the real damage came in the form of a continued blacklisting that affected Pete's livelihood all through the 1950s and into the next decade, and had collateral effects for his wife and children, as well as his siblings. The whole family came under sustained scrutiny. Job offers were rescinded, passports were denied.

Anthony Seeger, the son of Pete's older brother John, remembers the atmosphere at the time as tense. "When I was about 7 years old, I was playing a recording of the Almanac Singers, and I was playing a union song, and my father came storming into the room — it was a hot summer day — and threw the window shut and said, 'Don't you ever play that again with the window open.'"

But Anthony credits the experience with helping to inspire his own career as a musicologist. "I decided if music was so important that it was that scary, it must be really interesting," he explains. And in a lot of ways those trying years were similarly clarifying for Anthony's uncle. "For Pete, despite all the evidence to the contrary, the blacklist was the making of the man," Dunaway says. "Pete Seeger set himself up to be someone who could stand up and speak out, at a time when most Americans who disagreed with the domestic civil war against liberals called the Cold War could not speak out. He set himself up as someone who would not shut up, who would stand tall. And he did those things. And those are the moments that he is happiest about. Those are the moments that stand out in his mind as triumphs."

PETE'S YOUNGER HALF-SIBLINGS were at the time beginning to take their own, somewhat quieter paths. Mike and Peggy had grown up taking for granted the folk music that had taken their parents years to discover. "Our parents basically only sang these songs with us," says Mike, who is now 76. "I have a recording of me when I was about 5 singing 'Barbara Allen' and things like that."

With the model of his mother's transcriptions and the Lomaxes' field recordings close at hand, he developed a sense of music as something that needed to be preserved and protected. "When I started recording, because I just thought that was what should be done for kinds of music that hadn't been recorded before, I didn't exactly know what use would be made of it," he says. "Elizabeth Cotten, who was the first person I ever recorded, I didn't know why I was recording her. But then she got a Grammy."

According to well-worn family lore, Cotten was hired as the family's housekeeper after rescuing a lost Penny Seeger in a department store in 1948. When the family discovered that she also played guitar and sang, she became part of their extended musical project. Mike, who was learning to play and sing himself, began recording her songs when he was a teenager. Her first album came out on the Folkways label in 1957. (The Grammy came much later, in 1984, for a live recording.) Mike would record and produce others over the next few decades — maybe most notably, he tracked down Dock Boggs and all but single-handedly restarted his musical career. But he also became known for his own talents as a player and singer, which he put almost exclusively at the service of traditional material.

Newport, 1965: The New Lost City Ramblers, with Mike Seeger at center. Photograph courtesy Mike Seeger.

"I'd decided somewhere around 1955 that I didn't want to play city folk music," he says. "I wanted to play traditional music, maybe some bluegrass, but I didn't want to play urban folk music. It just didn't feel right. I was getting ready to go to electronics school so that I could go to the south, live in the south and just play music there. Then John Cohen and Tom Paley, just as I was coming back to old-time music, we got together and played music, and just one thing led to another."

What it led to was the New Lost City Ramblers, who, from their black-and-white album-jacket photos to their uncompromising arrangements, set themselves up against the prevailing trends toward Kingston Trio-style folk-pop. "We realized that we wanted it to be kind of a mission," Mike says. "We weren't real diplomatic about it, and I think we scared a lot of people who were thinking that they were just commercial."

One of the most striking accounts of Mike Seeger's skills and presence in that era comes in Bob Dylan's imagistic memoir, *Chronicles Volume One*, in which Dylan recalls seeing him play at Alan Lomax's downtown Manhattan loft in the early 1960s. "Mike was skin-stinging,"

(Above) *Alexia Smith and Mike Seeger, at their home in Alexandria, Virginia, July 2003. Photograph by Aldo Mauro. (Below) Peggy Seeger and Ewan MacColl at the Newport Folk Festival, 1960. Photograph courtesy Peggy Seeger.*

Dylan writes. "He was tense, poker-faced, and radiated telepathy, wore a snowy white shirt and silver sleeve bands. He played on all the various planes, the full index of the old-time styles, played in all the genres and had the idioms mastered." He concludes, "What I had to work at, Mike already had in his genes, in his genetic makeup. Before he was even born, this music had to be in his blood."

Meanwhile, Peggy was in England, where she had ended up after some time on the Continent. She had been hitchhiking around Europe, and in the spring of 1956 received a phone call while at a youth hostel in Denmark from Alan Lomax, whose intersections with the Seegers at key points seem almost supernatural. "He was a catalyst," Peggy says of Lomax. "He made people meet people. He made things happen." What he made happen in this case was the recruitment of Peggy for a British television production of the play *Dark Of The Moon*. "They needed a female singer who could also play the banjo," she says. "So I got on a train and went round to the Hook of Holland, and over to England for the first time. And in the meeting with the producer of that program, that was where I met Ewan MacColl. And that sealed my fate for the next 30 years."

MacColl was 20 years older than her, and married to the dancer Jean Newlove (mother to his son, Hamish, and his daughter, the late singer Kirsty MacColl). But he was so smitten that he famously wrote "The First Time Ever I Saw Your Face" for Seeger to perform. (In 1972, Roberta Flack had a #1 hit with it, and MacColl won a Grammy for Song of the Year.)

Peggy Seeger, 2004. Photograph by Irene Young.

They married in 1959, and were together until MacColl's death in 1989.

"We were a perfect match," she says, wryly. "I was American, he was English. Naturally, female and male, 21 and 41. I was literate in music and he was not — he wrote the most wonderful things, but couldn't read music. He was working-class, I was middle-class to intelligentsia class. He could play no instruments at all, but could sing wonderfully unaccompanied, and I played six."

But there were commonalities, and not only in their shared love of music. MacColl had been a political activist from his teenage years onward, and had been monitored for twenty years by MI5, the British domestic intelligence service. He was naturally sympathetic to Pete Seeger's legal travails, and when Pete played in London in 1961, while his case was still under appeal, MacColl served as chairman of the national "Pete Seeger Committee."

B Y THE TIME TAO Rodriguez-Seeger got to know his grandfather, most of the controversies that had attended to him for so long had faded into what, by the 1970s, seemed like the distant past. Pete was the old folksinger who had written Peter, Paul And Mary's hit "If I Had A Hammer," the reactionary who had, according to legend (Pete denies it to this day), tried to shut down Bob Dylan's electric rock 'n' roll performance at the 1965 Newport Folk Festival. To Tao, who spent his early years living near his grandparents in the Hudson River Valley, he was a companion and playmate.

"My grandpa and I are particularly close," he says. "I'm the oldest grandchild, so when I came along I think I was a bit of a novelty. He and I just gravitated toward each other. He likes to tell stories, so he told me stories, and he played me music. And I loved songs, I loved stories. I loved him. He'd put me to bed pretty much every night, with his banjo. I'd say, 'Sing me the one about the girl who kills herself because the guy won't love her.' And he'd go, 'Which one? There's plenty of them.'"

But in the late 1970s, Tao, who was born in 1972, moved to Nicaragua with his parents. His father, a Puerto Rican filmmaker, was invited by

Pete Seeger and Tao Rodriguez, undated promotional photograph.

the Sandinista government to document their revolution. Nine years of living in and around Managua had a profound effect on Tao's view of the world in general, and the United States in particular. More than any of the Seegers before him, he learned to see his native country as something like the enemy; Pete had been under surveillance, but Tao grew up under siege. "Every time I'd come back, which was rare, I was just shocked and appalled at how little people knew about what was going on," he says. "How little people knew about anything. People would say, 'Gee, you live in Nicaragua? What's it like living in Africa?'"

Returning to the States as a teenager, he spent some time learning to play guitar, and sort of naturally if not exactly intentionally ended up playing with his grandfather, and then accompanying him on his frequent tours and working holidays to one event or another. "I spent thirteen years, as I jokingly call it, as a professional grandson," Tao says. "I had no other musical outlet other than playing music with my grandpa." It didn't start out as a career, but eventually he realized that's what it was becoming. "I learned a hell of a lot," he says. "I have a pretty wide repertoire, because of the songs I learned over the years."

Looking for an outlet of his own, he turned to his friends Sarah Lee Guthrie (daughter of Arlo) and Johnny Irion; they played together for a couple years around the turn of the century as a folky trio called RIG, before Guthrie and Irion (who married in 1999) began playing and recording as a duo. Wanting to form another band, "a bigger, louder band," Tao founded the Mammals with Michael Merenda and Ruth Ungar in 2001. They played hard-charging folk-rock, setting both original and traditional songs to roaring fiddles and rattling drums. It gave Tao the outlet he was looking for. But after six years, four albums and very little money, the band went on hiatus. More recently, Tao has been performing with Pete again, most notably joining him and Bruce Springsteen to sing "This Land Is Your Land" for the Obama family at the Lincoln Memorial in January. ("Barack Obama signed my guitar," Tao says. "That's pretty cool.")

"I've really enjoyed this last year and a half, getting to play together again," he says of his grandfather. "I think it all has to do with discovering who you are, so there's no question of being sucked into the larger black hole that is him. His gravitational force is intense, and it will suck you in if you're not careful."

The Mammals (l. to r.): Jacob Silver, Rugh Ungar, Tao Rodriguez-Seeger, Michael J. Merenda Jr., and Chris Merenda, 2005. Photograph by Jayne Toohey.

To balance that out, Tao has been recording a solo album — a loud one. "I don't mind that he doesn't like rock 'n' roll," he says of Pete, "because it gives me something to have that he doesn't have."

if you're not careful." — Tao Rodriguez-Seeger

TAO WAS AT HIS GRANDFATHER'S side in May 2009 at Madison Square Garden for Pete's 90th birthday concert, which was staged as a benefit for Clearwater, an environmental and educational organization Pete established 40 years ago to lobby for a cleanup of the Hudson River. It is maybe Pete's most enduring cause, and is widely credited with helping to restore the once lamentable waterway to health. The lights onstage were arranged in the shape of a boat sail, mimicking the Clearwater sloop that Pete has for years used to ply the river and attract schoolchildren for lessons in freshwater ecology.

Tao Rodriguez-Seeger and Pete Seeger at Merlefest 2006, in front of a brick mural honoring Doc and Merle Watson. Photograph by Peter Blackstock.

Pete did not sing, but his speaking voice was strong, and he led the audience through several songs: "Amazing Grace," "This Land Is Your Land," and a warm rendition of "Good Night Irene" with Tao, Peggy, and Pete's older brother John, who was 95, chiming in. (Seeger men tend toward longevity; Charles Seeger died in 1979, at 92.)

Introducing "Amazing Grace," Pete told the story of the song's author, John Newton, an 18th-century British slave trader who underwent a religious conversion and became both a priest and, eventually, an abolitionist. "John Newton showed that you can turn your life around," Pete said. "And he gave all of us hope that we can turn this world around."

Then he gave the audience a brief lesson in harmony, humming different notes for each section of Madison Square Garden to sing. He encouraged crowd members to experiment and find something that sounded good to them. But before he started in with the words, he gave a final disclaimer. "There's no such thing as a wrong note," he said, "as long as you're singing."

Jesse Fox Mayshark lives in New York City. The first concert he ever saw was at the age of 5, when his parents took him to see Mike Seeger.

HARMONY

An oral history of two generations of **MAINES BROTHERS** bands, and the third-generation

& ENERGY

songstress who followed their lead   by **DON McLEESE**   photograph by **JOHN CARRICO**

What's in a name? Many music fans associate the Maines family name primarily with Lloyd Maines, who came to prominence in the 1970s as steel guitarist with the Joe Ely Band and has since established himself as one of the leading producers in Texas. Many more associate the name with Natalie Maines, Lloyd's youngest daughter, whose voice has brought the Dixie Chicks to multiplatinum stardom.

Yet those who live in Lubbock might well know the name as that of a popular band of the 1980s, the Maines Brothers Band, who try to reunite on at least an annual basis and who continue to sell CDs through their website. Though their sound is more mainstream than Lloyd's work with Ely (and many of the other artists he produces), with a hint of Alabama in

their vocal harmonies, their dynamic live performances and their dips into the Terry Allen songbook (Allen's "Amarillo Highway" is one of the band's signature tunes) are far more west Texas than Nashville.

And before Lloyd and his brothers Steve, Kenny and Donnie were the Maines Brothers Band, they were making music as the Little Maines Boys, because their dad and uncles were the original musical Maines Brothers, a dancehall favorite throughout the west Texas region in the 1960s. The Maines Brothers would let the Little Maines Boys, or the Little Maines Brothers, sing a few songs with them, and later open for them before the brothers were in high school. It wasn't until the original Maines

Above: An early portrait of the Maines Brothers Band, swiped from the cover of their avidly collected In Person album. At left: Lloyd Maines and friend, spring 2009. Photograph by John Carrico. Previous page, the Maines Brothers in person, March 1, 1986.

Brothers quit playing that the younger generation dropped the "Little" and took the name.

The Maines Brothers Band subsequently extended the same sort of opportunity to Natalie, who first sang to audiences at the invitation of her dad and uncles. And now that Natalie is a mother — as are her bandmates — it would be no surprise to see the next generation of the musical Maines family debut onstage with the Dixie Chicks. It was the recruitment of Natalie Maines by Dallas-based sisters Martie Maguire and Emily Robison that turned the trio from a retro cowgirl novelty act into the most popular (and, later, most controversial) band in country music.

The stir following Natalie's anti-George Bush remarks a few years back has been well-documented (and proved prescient), so we agreed from the outset that this would not be a story about those matters — though the support of a loving, loyal (albeit conservative Republican) family never wavered. This story is ultimately as much about the strength of those blood ties as it is about music.

"So we formed a band, and I was the oldest at 14. And we started playing

THE ORIGINAL MAINES BROTHERS AND THE LITTLE MAINES BOYS

LLOYD: My dad [James] started playing acoustic guitar back in the '60s. My first relative who made somewhat of a living making music was my uncle, Wayne, and he played upright bass with High Pockets Duncan. High Pockets was the guy who gave Waylon Jennings his first job at a radio station and helped encourage Buddy Holly. He was a real driving force in the West Texas music scene for a long time.

And then my dad and my other uncle Son — his name was Raymond, but they called him Son — took an interest in it and they were all really good singers. At family gatherings they'd always play. It was old-time country stuff, and that was our first exposure. And they always surrounded themselves with great local players, which inspired me and made me want to learn a lot of that stuff. So they started a band and just called themselves the Maines Brothers. Mainly just weekenders, because they all had other jobs. But they really became a popular band in the '60s around the dancehall circuit there.

Above: The Maines Brothers Band, grown up to be Polygram recording artists.

Back in those days, Lubbock was a dry town, so they played a lot in Post, which was about 30-40 miles east-southeast of Lubbock. And they would also play out at the old Cotton Club that Tommy Hancock owned at the time.

KENNY: Some of the very first memories I have as a child are of my dad and his brothers at our family gatherings, whether that be gathered around our kitchen table or the living room on a Sunday afternoon. I couldn't have been more than 3 or 4 years old.

STEVE: When I think back to the very first time of being interested in music, it was almost like it was simultaneous with Lloyd and Kenny and me. We'd be playing out in the front yard and there'd be music going on in the house. We'd pick up a shovel or a hoe or whatever and fake like we were playing. And I'm talking about when we were 3 and 4 years old. We were trying to emulate what our dad and uncles and all their friends were doing.

KENNY: There's a recording of Lloyd singing when he was 4 or 5 years old. And if I can get a hold of it I'd be happy to send it to you, just to blackmail Lloyd. He was singing the old rhythm & blues song "Mississippi Bullfrog." Anyway, it started with all of us at a very young age.

LLOYD: We were just skinny, awkward little kids with burr haircuts. And my dad would take us to these gigs and put us up onstage. We knew a lot of old, old country-type stuff. He'd let us sing a couple songs with the band, and the crowd thought it was really cool. So it perked our interest — it was really cool to go to a honky-tonk and go sing for a bunch of drunks. They weren't all drunk, but for a bunch of kids, it was an exciting time.

KENNY: I'm the third brother. Lloyd and then Steve and then me and Donnie. One evening after our dad came home from work — he worked as a mechanic in Slayton — my mom informed him

every honky-tonk in the area." — Lloyd Maines

we had been singing, so he got out his guitar and had us sing a couple songs that we'd been singing along to the record player for the past week or so. And he had us sing those two songs, probably for a couple hours, just over and over.

STEVE: Then Lloyd, being the oldest, he started learning chords on the guitar. He was a little bigger and he could handle our dad's guitar better than Kenny or I could. And all this time Donnie was five years younger than me, so he was a little further behind as far as getting in the mix. So Lloyd learned chords first, and then he taught Kenny and me. Then the interest level started picking up. I think Lloyd just has a God-given talent for being a music genius. For a long time he just played the lead guitar, and then he switched over and started messing with the steel guitar.

LLOYD: When I was in about the eighth grade, I bought a guitar chord book and started learning how to play acoustic guitar, just rhythm, and then I taught my brothers to follow along. And then Kenny decided that he would try bass. So this was all happening when I was about 14, Kenny was like 11, Steve was 12. Donnie, who later became the drummer, was way too young to even think about it. But us older guys had a friend of ours who played drums and had a fiddle player around.

So we formed a band, and I was the oldest at 14. And we started playing every honky-

Lloyd Maines, producing a smile. Photograph by John Carrico.

tonk in the area. And people would hire us because they knew my dad, they knew my uncles, they knew that we had their permission. As long as we didn't drink in the clubs. And, man, we had a big following. We just did a bunch of old Bob Wills, Ray Price, Johnny Bush, Merle Haggard songs. It was primarily dance music, but people just ate it up. Because we were just a bunch of kids up there, playing something other than rock 'n' roll, Beatles stuff. Which at that point we really hadn't been exposed to that much rock. And when the Beatles hit, they hit Lubbock about six months later than everywhere else.

STEVE: Our dad's name is James and then his brother just younger, Wayne, he was a bass player. And he had an electric bass and amp, and he'd quit playing and left it with us. And I don't know how it happened, but Kenny migrated over to bass, and he started messing with that and became the bass player. And I continued playing rhythm guitar. And how did Kenny end up being the lead singer? Beats the dog outta me. I enjoyed singing harmonies, and Lloyd enjoyed singing, but not that much, so it was like OK, Kenny, you take the leads here.

LLOYD: They called us the Little Maines Brothers, just so they wouldn't get us confused with my dad's band. And for about two years there, my dad and our uncles would play every Sunday night at the Cotton Club from like 8-12, and we would play like from 4-7. So we had a steady gig there when I was in high school and the other guys were in junior high. We just had a ball doing that. And we really honed in on our chops.

THE MAINES BROTHERS BAND

KENNY: I don't even know that billing is the right term. They were the Maines Brothers and so we were the Little Maines Boys, so as not to confuse people. And we remained the Little Maines Boys or Little Maines Brothers until I had just gotten into high school, and my dad had decided to leave the band. And at that point we took over the name, around 1968.

STEVE: Once we started playing the instruments, as fate would have it, the guy who was playing fiddle with our dad at the time had a son who was playing fiddle. He was our age and so we started messing around playing music with him. And the guy who was playing drums for our dad had a nephew who played drums. And he became our drummer. We had a five-piece group, and played our first paying gig in Slayton, Texas, which is about 18-20 miles outside of Lubbock. It was a VFW dance. We were in junior high at that point in time, and we were known as the Little Maines Brothers, because our dad and his brothers were the Maines Brothers. And we carried that name for several years, and then once our dad and his brothers stopped playing, we were able to move up and take over the big name. And then when we started doing our recordings around 1978 and added the other guys in the band who still play with us today, we became the Maines Brothers Band. Because it was more than just the brothers, it was the band that went with us.

LLOYD: Not until I was 16 or 17 did I get a steel. Until then I was playing really bad electric. But you know little kids doing what we were doing was such an unusual thing that we could kind of get by with the bare necessity talent. I mean, I played enough electric to make it sound authentic. And then the steel player from my dad's band, his name was Frank Carter, had a homemade steel he had been building for himself, but then he kind of aborted the project. But he had it built enough to where it could play. And I was at football practice one afternoon and came home and it was set up in the living room. He said, "Take it. It's yours."

So I started messing with it. There were really no teachers back then. It was just kind of figure it out for yourself. When I think back on it, I think that attributes to the style that I have. I don't really play like anybody else, and maybe that's because I had to work it out for myself. Frank did show me a few things, but I just learned steel by watching intently anybody who would come to town.

The guy that I saw most of all was Jimmy Day, because by that point he was playing with both Willie Nelson and Johnny Bush. And Willie would come play the Cotton Club, back in '68 and '69, when Willie had the crew cuts and the leisure suits. And Willie didn't draw enough to make the $1,000 guarantee, so I remember the manager of the club trying to haggle him down. As a kid, that was a memorable thing — the fact that a guarantee wasn't always a guarantee. But it must have worked out, because Willie came back a lot. I would set up by the side of the stage and just watch every move that Jimmy Day made, every nuance. But I would watch anybody and everybody who came through.

KENNY: When I graduated high school, I got a job at a clothing store at South Plains Mall here in Lubbock, working for minimum wage which at that time was $1.60 an hour. And I discovered really fast that it took me a week there to make the same money that I was making in one night of playing music. So it wasn't a tough decision for me to decide what I wanted to at least attempt to do for my career.

LLOYD: My plans never concerned music. I was just playing because it was fun at the time. I never wanted to be a star or some great, acclaimed musician. My plans were to go to college, which I did, South Plains College and Texas Tech, and got married to Tina in the meantime. I was studying agriculture and had plans to work for the Forest Service. I was enamored with forestry. But we had our first child, and I was

From left to right: Jimmie Dale Gilmore, Lloyd Maines, Richard Bowden, and Terry Allen, in a Lubbock state of mind. Photograph by John Carrico.

trying to meet expenses, so I started playing a lot. I was playing probably 5-6 nights a week and learning my craft while I was going to school. And then I got a call to play steel guitar on an advertising jingle at Don Caldwell's studio. And I enjoyed that so much I started doing more sessions. The next thing you know I'd totally fallen in love with the recording aspect of it.

My brothers and I played until we all got out of high school. We never really disbanded, we just kind of went off to college, and Kenny got this gig with Kenny Vernon, who was kind of a Vegas country act, had a couple of semi-hit records. And I started working at Caldwell's studio in Lubbock, and during that time is when I met Joe Ely and started playing with him. So during the early '70s we really didn't play that much.

REUNITING AND RECORDING

KENNY: At that point Steve had left the band and was going to school in South Texas. Lloyd and I were still playing around, but I had the opportunity to go with a little lounge band in

Vegas and I ended up doing that for three years. Kenny Vernon was the artist, and he was on Capitol Records at the time. He just turned 70 this year, but he's been working with Merle Haggard on the road for the last three or four years. I worked with Kenny until the end of 1976 and then decided to come back to Lubbock. The brothers were still here, so we decided to regroup and start playing again.

I think all of us had gained more experience, as far as performing. I probably learned more in Vegas about showmanship and stage performance than I ever had working the dances in Lubbock. You've got to move around a little bit. Even if you're not in a great mood, when you take the stage you've got to act like you are and bring the crowd along with you. And of course Lloyd had been out with Ely for several years and learned a lot about not just doing cover tunes. And even when you do cover tunes, make them your own. So we started to develop our own sound with a West Texas flavor. And we'd all matured a little bit, and by that point Donnie, the youngest brother, had graduated high school and had been playing drums with a couple of bands here. So Donnie had had some experience and added that to the band.

The Maines Brothers Band, at Coldwater County.

JOE ELY: When I decided to put a band together, Lloyd was the first guy I got in touch with. He had been working at Caldwell Studios in Lubbock, so he had experience of putting things down on tape and actually building it. He knew what worked and what didn't. So we kind of applied that to our live show. Lloyd was always a big part of that whole process, because he knew what was going to take the chorus to a higher level. He just understood how a song is built from the ground up, which really taught me a whole lot.

LLOYD: Toward the end of the '70s, when Steve had gotten out of college and married and Kenny had come back to town, they just sort of regrouped, just the two of them, and started playing gigs as the Maines Brothers. And even though I was still with Ely, any time I was back in town I'd come out and play with them. By this time, our little brother Donnie had become a really solid drummer, so at times, on certain gigs, there were four of us. In the early '80s, after I'd toured all through the '70s with Ely — we hit the road hard, and I did the records with him and we did the Clash tour and all that — my kids, Kim and Natalie, were getting old enough to where I felt they needed me around more. When I told Joe I couldn't travel as much, he was totally cool, absolutely, and said when you can play, play, and when you can't, I understand. And it's kind of been that way ever since. I still play with Ely from time to time and I just produced the new Flatlanders CD [*Hills And Valleys*, released in March 2009].

KENNY: At what was probably the last Tornado Jam [an early-'80s outdoor music bash in Lubbock], the Ely band was in town and had been rehearsing, and we were playing this junior-senior

than I ever had working the dances in Lubbock." — *Kenny Maines*

prom out at the Cotton Club. About midnight, Ely shows up with Jesse Taylor, Jimmie Dale (Gilmore) and Butch (Hancock). And Terry Allen was there, and Linda Ronstadt came in. And they all got up onstage and started jamming with us. And these kids were blown away. They couldn't believe it that their prom night had turned into something like that. There couldn't have been more than a hundred people total at that dance. But within three or four years there were like 500 people who said they were there.

LLOYD: Actually, once Steve and Kenny and Donnie started playing together in the late '70s, we made a couple of records with a really small budget. I mean $4,000; that's what Nashville guys were spending on catering. But they were very popular records. One was just called *Maines Brothers And Friends*. And one was called *Route 1, Acuff*, and that's where we cut a couple Terry Allen songs, (including) "Amarillo Highway." And that's when we started to get really popular. There was a place in Lubbock called Coldwater Country, and we would play there on weekends, like a two-night thing, and there'd be a line for a block and a half around the building. It was just a popular time for that kind of music. We were doing country, but it was pretty aggressive country.

KENNY: I really credit Terry Allen as one of the key figures in the sound that we eventually came up with in the Maines Brothers. It's amazing how the timing works, but I came back in '76-'77, and it wasn't long after that Terry came into Don Caldwell's studio to do the *Lubbock (On Everything)* album. I'd been working as a studio bass player, and that was one of my first projects when I came back to town. Once we adjusted to Terry's writing and timing and attitude, we fell in love with it. And there were several of his songs we worked into our show. And people started hearing that stuff they'd never heard before, and they thought it was ours. We tried to credit Terry as much as we could, but Terry gave us a little bit different direction from the western swing we'd grown up playing.

That may have contributed to our downfall in the Nashville music scene. We had been a commercial country band, but when we met Terry Allen, and started hearing what he was doing, we changed. Our musical direction did. We'd always had a high energy, but with Terry we heard something we really liked about the way songs were put together. And Lloyd and Donnie and I were members of the original Panhandle Mystery Band, performing those songs with Terry. It was just so much fun. Maybe we should blame Terry for throwing us off the track.

LLOYD: So we made a name for ourself around in the region and did another record called *Hub City Moan*, where we recorded a couple more Terry Allen songs. And then we recorded one called *Panhandle Dancer*, which was a Kevin Welch song. We became friends with Kevin and recorded some of his music. And that's the one that perked the interest of Mercury-Polygram. And they sent a representative to see us play and see the kind of crowds we were drawing. They signed us for like a six-record deal, but after two records we just didn't hit it off with the Nashville scene at all. We toured heavy from about '83 to '86, '87. Bought a bus, toured coast to coast, and had a lot of good experiences. But by that time everybody had kids at home, and it just got tougher and tougher. Those two we did for Mercury-Polygram are probably our least favorite records. And it was no one's fault but our own. We were trying to make ourselves radio-

The Maines Brothers Band with Terry Allen (far left) on an early "Austin City Limits," 1984. Lloyd Maines is on guitar at center, in the striped shirt. Photograph by Scott Newton.

ready, and I think in doing so we might have sacrificed some of our musical integrity. We cut a few songs that we wouldn't have otherwise.

STEVE: You get into what's happening in Nashville and who their PR people are gonna push to the radio stations. And sometimes it was us, but more often it was not. And so after doing two albums with them and not making a whole lot of money — heck, we didn't really make any money off the records — we were having to travel all over the country. Great exposure, but exposure doesn't buy a whole lot of groceries.

LIKE FATHER, LIKE DAUGHTER

NATALIE: If you grow up the child of a doctor, then you sort of learn your way around the hospital. And if you grow up the child of a musician, you have an ear for music and songs and arranging. I just always felt that was embedded in me.

I was definitely aware that there was always music around and that everyone in the family could play something. And that that wasn't necessarily the same way in everyone else's family. I think there's a lot of genetics to it. It was just always there. It wasn't anything conscious. I was singing as soon as I was talking. My parents said I was singing at 2. That used

the hospital. And if you grow up the child of a musician..." — Natalie Maines

The Dixie Chicks on "Austin City Limits," 1999. Lloyd Maines is on steel guitar at the left; Natalie Maines is dead center. Photograph by Scott Newton.

to not mean a whole lot to me, but now that I have my own kids, (when they were) at 2, I was worried about their singing, wondering if they've got any Maines musical genes at all. But it's working out. They actually are musical.

LLOYD: She would go to our gigs at a really early age, when she was 4 or 5 years old. I remember we were doing this show at the Lubbock Civic Center and we were backing up this real eclectic fiddle player named Cecil Caldwell who would be doing this John Hartford-style clog dancing while he was fiddling. And Natalie was just this cute little 4-year-old girl with blond, curly hair. She was standing in the wings and Cecil went over and got Natalie by the hand and she joined in and just tore it up. She had no idea what she was doing; she'd never clogged in her life.

And she always enjoyed the festivities, coming to the gigs, even when she got older. I'm not so sure she liked all the music we were doing — she wasn't much of a country fan — but she appreciated what we did. By the time she got into high school, my wife and I could tell, man, this girl is a singer. Every little kid can sing, but she could sing harmonies with people when she was 5 years old. She just listened to so much stuff and absorbed everything. She knew every word, every nuance, to the entire *Grease* soundtrack. And the *West Side Story* soundtrack — she could sing Puerto Rican. She knew all the dialogue, all the songs, front to end, the guys' parts, the girls' parts. So we knew she had something early on. When she got older and was coming to our gigs, we'd get her up and have her sing some Bonnie Raitt, maybe a James Taylor tune. And the crowd would go nuts.

JOE ELY: I remember when Lloyd carried Natalie into the Cotton Club when she was about two weeks old. Just seeing this brand new little baby in this honky-tonk, but she was part of the family. And when Natalie started singing, and Lloyd realized she was really a singer, she used to sit in with our band and blow everybody away. By then she was in her teens. But the first time she sat in with us, I thought, wow, this is more than a hobby.

NATALIE: I was never scared. I probably got more shy about it when I was in high school. I needed to be cool, and getting up onstage with my dad wasn't necessarily the coolest. My friends were not into country music, and neither was I. I was into the Maines Brothers, but I never had the fear that some cute guy that I liked would be there and see me. Nobody I liked would be there. In high school I thought I was a hippie, and that's when I got into a lot of classic rock from the '60s and '70s, and James Taylor, Lenny Kravitz, Indigo Girls. And Maria McKee.

But I liked Kenny's voice and their arrangements. It was definitely rockin', especially for country music back then. Much more progressive than the stuff that was out on the radio at the time. And I did like to go see my dad play with Joe Ely — that was the cool band. Especially when I was 18 and could get into clubs on my own. And I loved all of Terry Allen's stuff and still listen to him all the time. I liked the humor, the satire, the quirkiness, the rawness — and lots of West Texas references. There's definitely a certain feel to the music that comes from here, and it's very lyrical, worth listening to the words.

LLOYD: She just knew she wanted to sing. She had no inkling where or with who. And as luck would have it, I'd been doing some work with the Chicks with their original singers. There used to be four of them, and they hired me to play steel. A lot of writers get this wrong and think I gave them a cassette pitching Natalie to them, which is absolutely wrong. I just gave them a cassette like I'd give you a cassette. Hey, check out my daughter! She's a pretty good singer here.

NATALIE: I had always been very impressed with Martie and Emily's talents, with the way they played their instruments. But we didn't know each other that well, and I moved to Dallas within the week. And did my first gig in two weeks, I think. They knew I wasn't into the cowgirl western swing thing, but they made me feel confident that that wasn't what they wanted to do anymore. And that was the case.

THE MUSICAL SPIRIT OF THE MAINES FAMILY

KENNY: When I think of the three generations, harmony and energy are really the keys. In Natalie's case, she isn't working with other family members, but with Martie and Emily, all three might as well have been sisters. They lived together for enough years that they really have a feel for one another. And the things that I remember most about hearing my dad and his brothers was their harmony singing. There's first, third and fifth in harmony parts. And to me that's the holy trinity. When you get those three together, it gives me chill bumps. And

when she was about two weeks old." — *Joe Ely*

that's where I think genetics plays a part. When we sing together, we have the same inflection, we have the same vibrato, and those harmony parts just blend together. And I equate that to a spiritual event.

STEVE: I think the real connection of the three — the original Maines Brothers, the Maines Brothers Band, and Natalie and the Dixie Chicks — is that all of our music has made people feel good. You talk about the sixth man on a basketball team or the twelfth man on a football team? Our extra person that made things happen was the fans. Because of their interacting with us, people filled the floor. And with our dad and his band, people came out to hear them because they knew they were gonna have a good time and feel a part of what was going on. And I think that's what Natalie and them brought to country music — their music involved people feeling like a part of what they were doing. Their music was greater than just them.

Natalie Maines as a Dixie Chick.

LLOYD: We all have sort of an independent streak. Believe me, my dad and uncles were all strong-minded guys, way independent, and I'm sure they passed that along to us. And when we were doing music, we did stuff off the beaten path. Even though we had steel guitar and fiddle, we played country music like a rock band would play it. We were independent enough to do what we enjoyed, and Natalie is definitely from that school. I can't say she got it from me or the brothers, but she knows to follow what feels right and not what some corporation or machine says to do.

NATALIE: There's always a family feel, a lot of camaraderie. One thing I learned from my dad was just to be humble. It was just a job that my dad had. It was never something to show off, so I never really felt special in that way. And just seeing him always be so humble and so nice — you know, Lloyd Maines doesn't have an enemy in the world unless it's been his choice. Everybody likes him. He's just a good guy. And I can't ever say enough about my dad and his talent, his ability. I truly think he's one of the greatest producers. But very underpaid — except by the Dixie Chicks! So, I've learned lots of things from him, but I'm glad I've learned to be humble. In this career, I think everyone gets humbled, even if they weren't in the beginning.

Don McLeese, a former ND *senior editor who teaches journalism at the University of Iowa, considers Lubbock, Texas, a source of boundless fascination — one of the most conservative and isolated cities in one of the country's most conservative states, yet a wellspring of radical creativity.*

SONS
OF THE PREACHER
MAN

LEGENDARY GUITARIST GARY DAVIS HAD NO CHILDREN, BUT HIS PRODIGIES BECAME HIS ARTISTIC PROGENY

by **JOHN MILWARD**
illustration by **MANDY KEAPHLEY**

Reverend Gary Davis, photograph by Stefan Grossman.

STEFAN GROSSMAN WAS a 15-year-old Brooklyn kid when he called up the Reverend Gary Davis in 1960 to ask about taking guitar lessons. "Sure," said Davis, "come up and bring your money, honey." The next Saturday, Grossman's father drove him to a section of the Bronx that looked as "bombed out as Dresden." Grossman found his teacher "in a three-room sharecropper's shack behind a burnt-out tenement," and says it was a revelation to see "a musical genius living in utter poverty."

It was also kind of exotic. "You could smell the cigar smoke," Grossman said. "And you could see a sign over the living room that said, 'No Smoking.' And here was this man laughing and telling stories, and at the same time you had Annie, who was this really wonderful grandma, who'd make sure you felt good. There was no rush. You'd just stay and listen and get hypnotized. So for me, who never had a grandfather, it filled an emotional vacuum. I loved going there. And they called me the Devil's Son, because I had my tape recorder, and would always be after him to play these blues songs."

The Reverend Gary Davis was a guitar virtuoso, arguably the most famous street singer in the history of blues, and a teacher of enduring renown. "We're the old blues guys now," said Roy Book Binder, "which is kind of pathetic." Book Binder and his peers were luckier; the blues

which is kind of pathetic." — Roy Book Binder

revival of the 1960s offered direct contact with some of the most accomplished players of Depression-era country blues. To study with Davis was to step directly into the folk tradition.

Grossman and David Bromberg were two of his best-known students. "One night in 1969," Bromberg remembers, "I was performing at the Gaslight and Stefan was doing a concert at the Washington Square Church. The Reverend went to see Stefan, and when the concert was over, he came down to

Above: A young David Bromberg. Below: A more recent image of Stefan Grossman.

the Gaslight. I saw him in the audience and talked about him, and then sang a song that had been inspired by one of his. When it was over, he stood up and delivered a sermon. I can't remember all of it, but I'll never forget the first two sentences: 'I have no children, but I have sons.' And at that time, and at that place, he was claiming me and Stefan."

Davis played father to many other guitar players who paid $5 for lessons that could stretch throughout the day. His recordings and performances during the 1950s and 1960s also spread his influence to players who never inhaled the secondary smoke of his White Owl cigars. The Grateful Dead found an early standard in "Death Don't Have No Mercy," and Hot Tuna anchored its ragtime and country blues repertoire with such Davis tunes as "Hesitation Blues" and "I Am The Light Of This World." Bob Dylan, Dave Van Ronk, and Ry Cooder were among those inspired by the propulsive swing and snappy syncopations of Davis instrumentals such as "Buck Dance," "Twelve Sticks," and "Cincinnati Flow Rag."

Bromberg even got the Reverend to teach him some less-than-holy blues. "I remember when he taught me the 'Maple Leaf Rag,'" said Bromberg, "he had words to go with it: 'Get it up, get it up, get it up in a hurry.' I also remember him singing, 'Old Aunt Diana, don't you know, used to give her two nickels just to look at her hole. Laid down old Diana on her back, gave me my two nickels back.'"

"The Reverend always carried a pistol, because playing out on the street,

But guitar licks and a fast wit weren't always enough for a blind street singer; Gary Davis also packed heat. "The Reverend always carried a pistol," said Bromberg, "because playing out on the street, he had a lot of guitars stolen from him. I remember one lesson in his basement; he pulled out his new BB pistol to show it to me, and started firing it off. BBs were ricocheting off all the concrete. It was a little scary."

"**P**LAY WHAT YOU KNOW," Davis told his students, including Woody Mann, who recorded his lessons, and included this quote on his *Stairwell Serenade*. "Play just what you know." Davis knew plenty. He was born in Laurens Country, South Carolina, on April 30, 1896. One of eight children, only two of whom survived childhood, he was blind at or near birth. ("According to the statement of my grandmother," he told folklorist Elizabeth Lyttleton Harold in 1951, "I had the sore eyes when I was three weeks old. And the doctors put something in my eyes that caused ulcers to grow over my eyes and caused me to go blind.") But he sure had ears. "The first time I ever heard a guitar played," he told author Sam Charters, "I thought it was a brass band."

Davis was playing guitar and singing in the Baptist church by the time he turned 8. Religion and music were his eyes on the world, and for the rest of his life, he used his guitar to spin spirited sermons. At 15, he began playing with a string band in Greenville, South Carolina, but he was by nature a loner, and spent most of his life playing as a solo street performer. By the early 1930s, he'd settled in Durham, North Carolina.

Rev. Gary Davis. Photograph by Stefan Grossman.

Fingerpicking guitarists from the southeast are said to play in the Piedmont style, a term that accommodated such distinct instrumentalists as Blind Blake, Josh White, Blind Willie McTell, and Blind Boy Fuller. Davis had a boisterous, fleet-fingered style that drew upon most every music that had crossed his path, including blues, jazz, gospel, parade marches, and popular tunes. But he probably owed the most to ragtime, the syncopated piano music that was popular in the early 20th century, and best known to contemporary listeners from "The Entertainer," the Scott Joplin tune popularized by the 1973 film *The Sting*. Had Joplin played guitar instead of piano, the foremost composer of ragtime might have sounded something like Gary Davis.

Davis made his first recordings in 1935, and the sessions included a pair of blues; he subsequently refused to perform anything but religious music. Over the years, he fudged on this *he had a lot of guitars stolen from him.”* — *David Bromberg*

pledge like a God-fearing man happy to savor a drink of whiskey. Yet his refusal to tailor his pastiche of styles to accommodate the blues market meant that he would make no new recordings (save two gospel tunes) until the mid-1950s.

But Davis was far from your typical rediscovered legend. He was ordained as a Baptist preacher in 1937 (the same year he married Annie Bell Wright), and shared a devotional musicality with Blind Willie Johnson, the scintillating, slide-guitar playing master of the holy blues. Both men had fiery fingers that played in service of the Lord. Davis carried himself with evangelical zeal, and welfare caseworkers were sometimes regaled with shouted sermons. One asked Davis to play his guitar. “His ability as a guitarist is unbelievable,” she said. “I have never heard better playing.”

Rev. Gary Davis, recording with Miss Gibson in the UK. Photograph by Robert Tilling.

Davis moved to New York City around 1940, performed on the streets of Harlem, and preached in storefront churches. Folklorists had to travel to the tiny Delta town of Avalon to find Mississippi John Hurt, and trailed Son House to Rochester, New York; in both cases, these fabled musicians had stopped playing the guitar. By contrast, Greenwich Village gumshoes had only to take the A-train to rediscover a street-singing Segovia who not only never stopped playing, but had gotten better.

Reverend Davis was most always dressed for church, the picture of righteousness in a suit and tie and bright white shirt. Dark aviator glasses, a fedora, and the big-bodied guitar he called “Miss Gibson” completed his street-musician style. Players who engaged him for lessons stepped right into history. “How are the great traditional musics of the world taught? By example,” said Grossman. “It's always the student imitating the teacher. There's nothing written, it's just passed from one to the other.”

For two years, Grossman spent his weekends soaking up all he could, documenting songs with his tape recorder, and working to master Davis' unique two-fingered picking style. (Most fingerstyle players pick with their thumb, index, and middle fingers. Davis used just his thumb and index, and told his students to approach the guitar as if it were a piano, with the thumb handling the left-hand bass part while the index finger sculpts the right-hand melody. His unique picking patterns also spiked his music with rhythmic “rolls.”) “I was trying to learn everything note for note,” said Grossman, “and for Davis, you need to use the two fingers to get the feel and syncopation right. And the more you tried to play exactly like him, the more he would show you, because he was very aware of the student-teacher relationship. He told me that I couldn't perform in public until he said it was OK. I said, ‘Why?’ And he said, ‘Because you're taking my name into the public.’”

Students brought Davis income and valuable support. Both Bromberg and Grossman accompanied the Reverend to music gigs both secular and sacred. “On Friday night, he'd come down to the Village and go to some coffeehouse and earn maybe a hundred bucks passing the hat,” said Grossman. “Saturday there might be a Bar Mitzvah, and you'd take him, not to the ceremony, but to entertain your Jewish friends. The parents loved him. Then on Saturday night, there'd be a concert at a college, and you'd find yourself eating with the president of Swarthmore, and the first thing Reverend Davis would do was take out his false teeth and put them on the table. Then he'd eat with his hands. Finally, on Sunday, he'd take us to a storefront church, with maybe fifteen people in the congregation, and you'd have him preaching, and then he'd get into a song and get the spirit. He doesn't get that spirit when he'd sing the song in front of a white audience at Gerdes. But in church, he'd go to places where I've never been."

The late Dave Van Ronk described a Reverend Davis church service in his memoir, *The Mayor Of MacDougal Street*: "His sermons were remarkable. He would set up a riff on his guitar, and then he would chant his sermon in counterpoint to the riff, and when he made a little change in what he was saying, he would make a little change on the guitar. There was this constant interplay and interweaving of voice and guitar, and these fantastic polyrhythms would come out of that — I have never heard anything quite like it, before or since."

"One of the things I learned from Reverend Davis was to let the guitar talk," said Bromberg, "and the whole idea came from hearing the Reverend let his guitar finish sentences for him."

JORMA KAUKONEN NEVER studied with Reverend Davis, though he did see him lay his hands on his Gibson J-200 in a Greenwich Village club. But at Antioch College, Kaukonen met Ian Buchanan, a gifted guitarist who taught him songs such as "Keep Your Lamp Trimmed And Burning," "Hesitation Blues," and "Sally Where'd You Get Your Liquor From." Nearly 50 years later, these Davis tunes are still active in his repertoire. Kaukonen's most recent album, *River Of Time*, includes another by Davis, "There's A Bright Side Somewhere."

"I think what drew me to these songs was the completeness of his guitar style," says Kaukonen. "And I also liked that his whole take on everything was rather upbeat, even though he might be singing about death. There was always an 'it's going to be all right' feeling about his music. You think about a man born the century before last, a blind black man in the south, and you think that after all the stuff that he endured, he still seemed to be a very powerful upbeat kind of guy."

Jorma Kaukonen (center) onstage at the Fur Piece Ranch. Photograph by John Flavell.

Kaukonen moved to California in the mid-1960s, taught guitar, and joined a band that became Jefferson Airplane. "I came to the Airplane totally unfamiliar with band playing, or playing rock 'n' roll," he said. "I used my fingers to play a lot of the leads, and that background gave me a different entree into playing rock 'n' roll."

While Kaukonen was becoming a rock star, Reverend Gary Davis was enjoying his first taste of worldly success, recording albums and playing at clubs and colleges, and appearing with other rediscovered bluesmen at the Newport

in counterpoint to the riff..." — Dave Van Ronk

Folk Festival. He also bought a home in Queens thanks to publishing royalties for songs he may or may not have written that were being sung by folk stars such as Peter, Paul And Mary and Joan Baez. "Peter, Paul And Mary wanted him to have the publishing royalties to 'If I Had My Way,'" said Ernie Hawkins, who studied with Davis in 1965, "and he and the group and his manager were all gathered in a lawyer's office and they asked him, 'Did you write this song?'

And Gary Davis said 'No.' There was silence, and then the Reverend said, 'The Lord gave it to me in 1927.' Coincidentally, that was when Blind Willie Johnson recorded it. So he had loopholes. He was a smart guy."

Hawkins once booked his teacher for a blues festival in his native Pittsburgh. "We had a couple of workshops with guys like Mance Lipscomb and Son House and Fred McDowell, and before long everybody was hanging around Gary Davis. He was like the king of these guys. They all respected the way he played, and he entertained them with jokes and stories. Victoria Spivey was there, and they started playing these old songs, with her singing and him playing. His guitar was deep and complex, and you could feel that this was where his heart lived."

Kaukonen and Jack Casady left the Jefferson Airplane in the early 1970s to focus on their coffeehouse band, Hot Tuna. "The Airplane thing was a blessing," said Kaukonen, "because it allowed me to be a better-than-decently-paid folk musician." 1970's Hot Tuna popularized Davis tunes that Kaukonen had learned

Rev. Gary Davis in performance. Photograph by Stefan Grossman.

back in college, including "Hesitation Blues" and "Death Don't Have No Mercy." Kaukonen used three fingers when he picked, which gave his Davis interpretations a folksier spin. "Anywhere you go in the world," says Hawkins, "somebody's going to be able to play 'I Am The Light Of This World' just like Jorma."

REVEREND GARY DAVIS continued teaching until long after the money really mattered. "I called him after finding his name in the phone book," said Ernie Hawkins, who moved to New York at age 18 with the express purpose of studying with Davis, "and found my way to a storefront on a busy street in Queens. He was asleep in the back. I stood there for a long time and finally touched him on the shoulder and he exploded and started yelling. So I ran back out onto the street."

Hawkins got up the nerve to go back inside and cough up $5 for the first of nearly a year of lessons. "When you could see him play, it really made a huge difference," said Hawkins, "because some of the stuff on his records is really difficult, if not impossible to figure out. He'd play these incredibly complex pieces, but he had a very economical style, and his hands hardly moved. I think it was a combination of intelligence and a great ear that let him figure out a style that had such range, and that allowed him to play in any key up and down the neck."

Roy Book Binder jokes that he was Reverend Davis' worst student, but after quitting college to go on the road with Davis in 1967, he also became one of his closest confidantes. Their first outing was a train trip to Chicago for a four-night stint at the Quiet Knight. "The guarantee was $400 versus fifty percent of the door," said Book Binder, "and the tickets were $1.75."

"I'd count the money after gigs and he'd tie it up with a string and stick it down his long johns," said Book Binder. "He didn't like to change clothes on the road. I'd say, 'Reverend Davis, this is Tuesday and Mother Davis said to put your brown suit on.' And he'd say, 'Where's Mother Davis?' 'She's back in Queens.' 'When we're on the road,' he'd say, 'we're on the road. I'm wearing the blue suit all week.'"

Book Binder, like all of Davis' traveling companions, had another important responsibility. "He liked the occasional shot of whiskey," said Book Binder, "and you'd have to be careful to intercept bottles that kids would try to pass along. Of course, I'd give him a glass. He'd say, 'Is there a phone call for me?' That was code for he wanted a drink. I'd go to the bartender and have him put a quarter inch of whiskey in the glass. And I'd come back and say, 'There's a call for you Reverend Davis.' And he'd say, 'Is it long distance or local?' And I'd say, 'It looks like a local.' And he'd say, 'OK, let me see it.' I never let him get near a long distance call."

Reverend Davis also had his favorite foods. "We'd go out to lunch," said Book Binder, "and he'd say, 'I'll have the pork chops.' And the waitress would say, 'Would you like peas or carrots with that?' And he'd say, 'Are the peas greasy?' And she said, 'Certainly not.' 'OK, then I'll have the carrots.' He liked all that greasy soul food crap."

Traveling can be tough on even the best of friends. "I might not talk to him for two weeks after a road trip," said Book Binder, "because sometimes it was like going on tour with your grandfather. I remember calling up the house, and I'd ask Annie how she was, and she'd say, 'Do you want to talk to the Reverend?' And I'd say, 'Not really.' But then I'd say, 'You ask him if he wants to talk to me.' And

Rev. Gary Davis, Roy Book Binder (center), and an unidentified fan, ca. 1968. Photograph courtesy the Robert Tilling collection.

she'd come back and say, 'He'll talk to you if you want to talk to him.' Then we'd finally talk, and everything would be fine."

Reverend Davis presided over weddings for, among others, Wavy Gravy (Dylan and Van Ronk were among those at the service singing "Just A Closer Walk With Thee") and Ernie

Hawkins. "He had a book with some Braille in it," said Hawkins, describing the ceremony in his Pittsburgh apartment, "but I didn't know whether he was actually reading it or just making it up. He said some words and gave us a little talk about being married. And then he said, 'OK, you're married.' Then he taught me 'Will There Be Any Stars In My Crown?' — that was my wedding present."

WOODY MANN STILL remembers Reverend Davis' phone number — AX1-7609. He first dialed it in 1968, when he was 12 years old. (Mann, 54, is the youngest of Davis' "sons," with Kaukonen the oldest at 68.) "I was looking for a guitar teacher," said Mann. "I remember asking Van Ronk and he said, 'Get out of here, kid.'" So he called every Gary Davis in the book, and eventually found the Reverend. His mom drove him from Long Island to the home in Queens. "When I arrived, I knew the name Gary Davis and that he'd written 'Candyman,'" said Mann. "So I got there, and he was having dinner, and putting his teeth away, this big ritual, and then he picked up his guitar and started playing in the living room, doing all sorts of amazing stuff. I said, 'What is that?' And he said, 'That's what you call ragtime.' And I said, 'Can I study with you?'"

Decades later, I studied with Mann when he was teaching guitar at the Augusta Heritage Festival in Elkins, West Virginia. Late one afternoon, on a porch overlooking a campus chapel, he played tapes from his four years of studying with Davis. The first one found the teenager confidently thumping through a ragtime instrumental; when he hit the second verse, however, the kid's guitar was comically overwhelmed by the powerful playing of the old master. On another tape, the Reverend sang a song for his young student — "I Will Do My Last Singing In This Land Somewhere" — and it occurred to me that I knew this deeply moving song from Davis' *Live At Newport*. Except that here, Davis was singing to an audience of one with the same spine-tingling passion that he'd summoned for the festival crowd.

"Reverend Davis would always put his all into whatever he was playing," said Mann. "When I was alone in his living room or would see him at a church or on the stage, if he'd play 'Samson & Delilah,' he'd play it with the same intensity."

Roy Book Binder says that Reverend Davis instantly recognized Mann as a prodigy. Mann remembers his teacher's determined persistence. "We'd go lick by lick through songs, and then maybe jam on it for an hour," said Mann. "He wouldn't move on before I got a part right. For 45 minutes we'd go over one verse, over and over. The guy had amazing patience."

Mann would go home with his recordings and polish each tune. "I'd go back the next week and play it for him," said Mann, "and then he'd play it completely differently. It used to drive me nuts. And that's when I realized that he was really all about improvising. He would play 'Hesitation Blues' for twenty minutes, not repeat himself, make the shit up as he goes, and his timing was always perfect. It was the first time I'd heard a fingerstyle guitar player not playing an arrangement, but improvising."

Mann continued his studies at the Juilliard School and with jazz pianist Lennie Tristano, but he remains captivated by the unique genius of Reverend Davis. "He was always very hard to categorize," said Mann, "which is why he's something of a footnote. Even in blues books, they just don't know where to put him. Davis didn't play blues, and his music had melody. He would harmonize gospel tunes in beautiful chordal ways, and nobody played that way, either before or after. But the drive to improvise and the sense of swing is what really got me. You're not learning a tune; you're learning how to play."

One Sunday, Mann went with Davis to a church service. "It was like in a condemned movie theater, with all these chairs thrown up in the balcony," Mann recalled. "The congregation filled the first two rows, and all the women were in their Sunday finery, with white gloves and hats and dayglo colors. And he was up there preaching and playing. And then he turned to me and said, 'Give us a song, boy.' I knew one song I could sing, 'Say No To The Devil.' It was funny, here I was a middle-class white kid, and I'm up there freaking out trying to play and sing. I wasn't even thinking about the lyrics; I was just worried about the guitar. I finally looked up, because my eyes were closed, and I'll never forget it. Nobody was looking at me. They all had their eyes closed, clapping their hands, rolling around in their chairs and singing along with me. And it was so cool that I got totally relaxed because I realized they don't care about me, and they weren't checking out my playing."

Then Davis came to Mann's house. "I asked Reverend Davis to do a concert at my house, and he went, 'Sure, just don't tell my manager.' It was an anti-Vietnam War thing, and he said, 'I'll support that. I'm against war.' My mother made brownies and cookies, and we picked him up, and put him in the living room. We had to pay him $300; I sold tickets and all the kids were on the floor. And he did a concert, and at one point, he even fell asleep."

Davis was a gifted sleeper. Van Ronk wrote of a late night drive from Boston to New York with Davis sprawled across the back seat picking "Candyman." "By New Haven it was really beginning to bug me, but what could I say? This was the Reverend Gary Davis playing 'Candyman.' Bridgeport, somewhere around Stamford, something inside me snapped. I growled, 'For Christ's sake, Gary, can't you play anything else?' And I turned around, and he was asleep."

Roy Book Binder never saw Davis play in his sleep. Still, he said, "He'd fall asleep all the time. We'd be in a lesson, and sometimes it was hard to identify the chord he was playing, so you'd walk around him to look at it from all angles. Then you'd go back in front of him and he'd be snoring."

"**M**OTHER DAVIS USED to have parties, and all the students would come over to the house," Book Binder reflected. "Reverend Davis would say, 'I'm just going to sit here and have everybody play the songs. You're coming to entertain me.' But when the first note was hit, he'd grab his guitar and be bashing along the whole time. He loved to play, and loved to interact with people, and his music let that happen."

Reverend Davis left a lasting impression on his sons. "He gave me direction and confidence," says Book Binder, "and showed me a way to have a traveling, creative life." For decades, Book Binder lived on the road, in a mobile home. These days, he's happy to have a wandering musician's best friend: a wife with a job and a house in Florida.

and nobody played that way, either before or after." — *Woody Mann*

It's no accident that many who studied with Davis teach guitar; fingerstyle guitar players typically work far from the musical mainstream. Stefan Grossman's Guitar Workshop markets instructional DVDs, books and recordings, and his catalogue includes works by Bromberg, Hawkins, Van Ronk, Book Binder, and Mann. He's also overseen such Gary Davis products as the *Demons And Angels* box set, a DVD of assorted videos, and a new collection (*Live At Gerde's Folk City*) of 1962 concerts that Grossman recorded when he was 17 years old.

Ernie Hawkins never put down his guitar, but he also earned a B.A. in philosophy and a Ph.D. in phenomological psychology. Still, music remained his calling. "For years," he said, "I tried to puzzle out what he'd taught me. By the '90s I realized that learning Gary Davis was a lifelong project, because the more I learned, the more I recognized how much depth was there. I realized that if I wanted to be more than a dilettante, I'd really have to keep devoting myself to digging deeper into what I'd learned, and what he could still teach me. It's almost like you can never quite get to the bottom of his music."

"For me, it was all about the cool guitar parts," said Mann, a working musician who gives guitar clinics around the world and is producing a documentary film about Davis called *Harlem Street Singer*. "I learned the lyrics, but I didn't really feel the spiritual aspects of the tunes, though I knew that he did. I'd be the only one in the house and he'd be crying and shouting and whooping and hollering. It was kind of scary, but also beautiful."

"I'm a Jewish guy who's learned all this Christian music," said Kaukonen. "I once talked to David [Bromberg] about how the Reverend's music transcends a belief in Jesus Christ as a living God. David said, 'Jesus was a great Rabbi,' and that's as far as he goes. But the music transcends all that stuff, and the metaphors that the Reverend used work just fine for me."

Between concert tours, Kaukonen teaches guitar at his own Fur Peace Ranch, a high-end guitar camp in southeastern Ohio. "I love teaching people who are interested in this odd little corner of the musical universe," says Kaukonen, "and it makes me a better player." The average student is a middle-aged professional with a fine guitar; they sign up to study with Kaukonen and other teachers, including (at various times) all of Gary Davis' musical sons. "Gary Davis Weekend" is a regular feature at Fur Peace Ranch, which is a long way from a humble home in Queens, let alone a shack in the Bronx. But all the same, a singular tradition is being shared, passed, and preserved.

"The last time I saw him was in the hospital," said Roy Book Binder. The year was 1972, and Davis was 76. "He weighed maybe 90 pounds, and I'm holding his hand, and he didn't have his glasses or his teeth. It was like death. I said, 'Reverend Davis, besides the music, my entire circle of friends, and everybody I know, came from you.' And he said, 'I know.' He knew he was the best. And I believe he was the best because God gave him the ability to convert souls with his music. And in a way, we were all kind of converted."

John Milward has written about music and popular culture for more than 30 years. He expects to be refining his interpretations of "Cincinnati Flow Rag" and "Buck Dance" until death don't have no mercy.

THE
IMPORTANCE
OF BEING

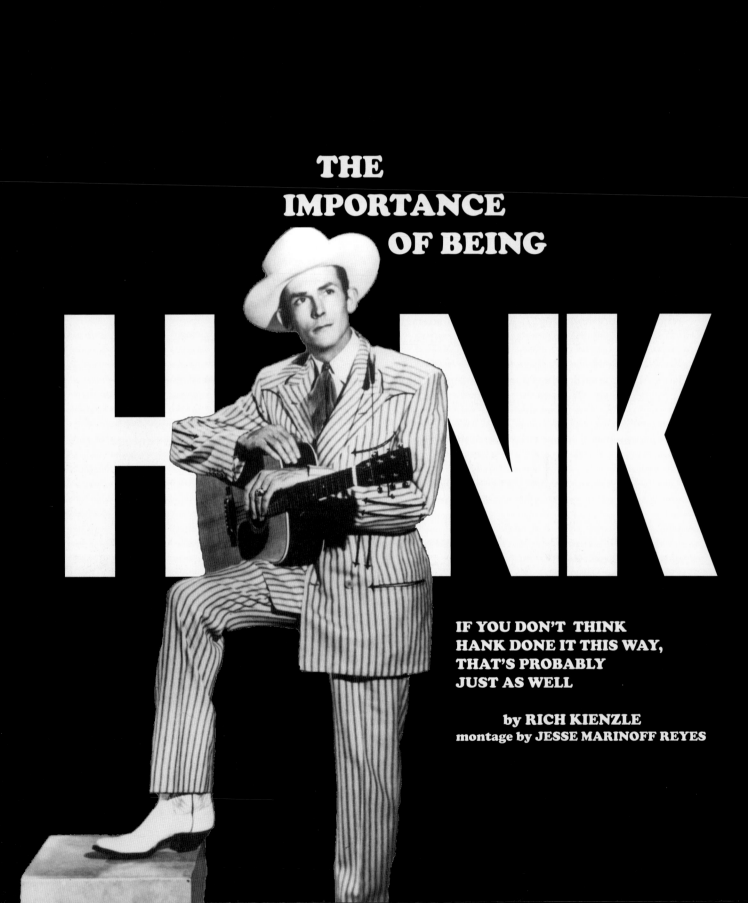

HANK

**IF YOU DON'T THINK
HANK DONE IT THIS WAY,
THAT'S PROBABLY
JUST AS WELL**

by **RICH KIENZLE**
montage by **JESSE MARINOFF REYES**

"Stated simply, nobody wins here. Too many have tinkered with Hank Senior's recorded legacy since he died, so he didn't need this. As for Bocephus, he ought to quit resting on his laurels (and his Monday Night Football fame) and get back to creating the vital, visceral music he excelled at 15 years ago. The only unscathed person here is Hank III, whose promising talents deserve exploration on a full-length album, not this overhyped, underwhelming Nashville studio stunt."

That was the closing paragraph of a review I wrote nearly fourteen years ago of an album titled *Three Hanks: Men With Broken Hearts* for the January-February 1997 issue of *Country Music* magazine. The album, Hank III's introduction to the world, was one more exercise in the fine art of Hanxploitation (my term), the cynically contrived studio gimmickry designed to remarket Hank Sr. and his progeny to a new audience, with a (mercifully) small bit of his wife Audrey thrown in for good measure. The review pissed off a few readers, which bothered neither my editors nor me, since it happened all the time.

It wasn't the temerity of the *Three Hanks* concept that bothered me. Since Hank Sr.'s final Cadillac ride in 1953, MGM and their successor labels have done their damnedest to keep him relevant by harnessing state-of-the-art technology of every era, standard practice for best-selling, deceased recording artists of any genre. MGM President Frank Walker got the ball rolling not long after Hank's death by having the Drifting Cowboys and session players over-dub spiffy accompaniment onto solo acoustic material, both demo recordings and Shreveport radio performances. The advent of stereo brought an idea even more half-assed: improving the fidelity of Hank's classics, all recorded in mono, by clumsily dubbing on percussion and other instruments to give it a stereo feel. It came off sounding weird. RCA followed a similar routine after Jim Reeves died a decade later.

Unwilling to allow the smooth "countrypolitan" market of the mid-'60s to render Hank (or his record sales) irrelevant, they addressed the issue with three vile, unlistenable *Hank Williams With Strings* albums. The fun with overdubbing didn't end there. With Hank Jr.'s mid-'60s recording debut, it was no surprise that MGM issued two creepy-sounding *Father And Son* "duet" LPs which foreshadowed later studio hijinks. They fared better letting Junior "finish" song fragments Hank left behind and record the fully-formed tunes himself; his 1969 hit single "Cajun Baby" remains one of his better early recordings. "Credit" for all this goes to Frank Walker's nephew, MGM executive and ex-insurance broker Jim Vienneau.

All this forced musical amity obscures both the commonality and divergence between the three Williams generations — Hank Sr. to Hank Jr. and Jett to Hank III and half-sister Holly. Time's march has affected every succeeding age bracket differently as they've found themselves, as Junior wrote, "standing in the shadows." Those variations, reflecting over six decades of profound change in country music and in America itself, affected the niches each carved for themselves. To examine it all, we may as well start at the source.

HANK
Growing up with his divorced mother Lilly in Alabama, Hank always had a taste for the gutbucket. Certainly he didn't absorb it from his seldom-seen daddy Lon, who played a Jew's harp. It was Lilly, a church organist, who made sure he learned the shape-

between the three Williams generations..."

HANK WILLIAMS   exclusively on   M-G-M Records

note singing that infused his later gospel performances with a bracing, even chilling fervor. In those early years of hillbilly recording, Jimmie Rodgers, who influenced nearly everyone, barely left a mark on Hank. Riley Puckett was another matter, for Hank almost surely heard at least two of the Atlanta singer-guitarist's discs; the couplet often quoted as an early idea ("I had an old goat/She ate tin cans/When the little goats came/They were Ford sedans") actually came from "Slim Gal," a 1928 Puckett-Clayton McMichen recording. It's well known that "W.P.A. Blues," the "original" which helped a young Hank win an amateur show, was a knockoff of Puckett's 1930 "Dissatisfied."

Alabama bluesman Rufus Payne, better known as Tee-Tot, was part of both the life and legend. There's little doubt Payne cultivated a feel for blues in the gangly, big-eared Hank, and it never left him. He likely learned the Clarence Williams tune "My Bucket's Got A Hole In It" from Payne, along with the bluesy guitar licks Hank incorporated into his MGM recording of it (his only recorded guitar solo). As later happened with his son and grandson, he clashed with the suits over the song — in this case, Fred Rose, Hank's mentor and independent producer. No slouch himself as a composer, Rose so detested "Bucket" that he walked out while Hank recorded it. The song caused similar friction with another set of suits: those running the Opry. Forbidden to sing the line "I can't buy no beer" onstage, he sarcastically shouted "Milk!" at the strategic spots. And contrary to the bullshit screen play of the 1964 Hank biopic *Your Cheatin' Heart* starring George Hamilton, Tee-Tot did not die in young Hank's arms.

Hank's love for Bob Wills and dance music is a given. In the '40s he hung out with Pappy Neal McCormack's country dance band around Pensacola, Florida. Drifting Cowboys steel guitarist Don Helms, who joined Hank in 1943, told me in the 1980s that for dancehalls, the band added drums, horns and piano, Hank tearing loose with "Matchbox Blues" and other raw fare that actually anticipated Junior's later material. That side rarely surfaced on his records, except for an occasional jumper such as "I'm Satisfied With You" or "Fly Trouble," commercial flops recorded at Rose's urging. His spiritual and musical impact on early rock is a given, and there's little doubt that "Move It On Over," Hank's adaptation of an old twelve-bar blues, weighed heavily on the minds of the two songwriters who composed the Bill Haley anthem "Rock Around The Clock."

But as Hank readily admitted, Roy Acuff was his first true idol, his Holy Grail. From the time Acuff joined the Opry in 1938, his cathartic, keening vocal style — blasted across the continent over WSM, heard on stages around the nation, and played on platters flying out of record stores — clearly spoke to rural Americans who'd contended firsthand with the Depression, in a day when no middle class existed and music was largely a haven from the harsh problems of everyday life. He deeply influenced Hank's singing and early approach, apparent in the World War II-themed composition "(I'm Prayin' For The Day That) Peace Will Come," which he sold to Pee Wee King in 1943. Interviewed by San Francisco jazz writer Ralph Gleason in 1952, Hank waxed eloquent about Acuff's unabashed sincerity, lauding the way he'd "stand up there singing, tears running down his cheeks." All these influences and Hank's own genius led to his epochal body of work, one that proved a blessing — and to some degree a curse — for his descendants.

true idol, his Holy Grail."

HANK JR.
Pictured below is a nonexistent 45 disc from a satirical rare-record auction list I created in the 1980s and circulated among record-collector friends. Like most satire, it contained a glimmer of truth in the battles that Randall Hank Williams, a.k.a. Hank Jr., a.k.a. Bocephus, had to fight on two fronts: his daddy's legacy, and his mother Audrey's obsessive control over his musical destiny. It took him years to overcome both and succeed on terms of his choosing.

Audrey, despite her wealth from Hank's songwriting royalties, quickly became an even bigger pain to her son than she'd been to her husband. Having deluded herself into thinking she advanced Hank's career, the widow grew fixated on creating new stars — Junior among them. He was in grade school when he first sang onstage, needing only to do as Mama said: Sing a Hank tune and watch the crowds cheer and bawl. When he signed with MGM at 14, he didn't start at the bottom of the label roster. Instead, he recorded the

I AIN'T GONNA SING NO MORE OF DADDY'S SONGS/YOU WIN AGAIN

Hank Williams Jr.

soundtrack album to *Your Cheatin' Heart*, the fanciful biopic that made *Walk The Line* look like a documentary by comparison.

Junior's first hit single was a 1964 cover of "Long Gone Lonesome Blues," and nearly every one that followed (except for his awful duets with pop chanteuse Connie Francis) had a Hank connection. Among the worst: his 1966 original "Standing In The Shadows," a Hanked-up rendition of Jody Reynolds' pop necro-fantasy "Endless Sleep," and 1968's "I Was With Red Foley (The Night He Passed Away)," a Luke The Drifter-style recitation released, not surprisingly, under the name "Luke The Drifter, Jr." Foley, Hank's Opry buddy, who sang "Peace In The Valley" at Hank's funeral as he'd promised to, took a more circuitous path to alcoholic oblivion; he checked out in an Indiana motel room while touring with Junior fifteen years later.

For Junior, all this gradually became a royal pain. Straying too far from the Hank party line upset both his audiences and MGM. Another problem: Replicating the famous Hank vocal twang forced his natural baritone into a higher, less comfortable vocal register that often sent him sliding off pitch, something his uncritical fan base never noticed. His band, of course, was named "The Cheatin' Hearts." Clever. Oh, and Jim Vienneau was still producing.

Like his dad, Junior favored gutbucket fare, albeit a broader range reflecting their age differences. He loved both the early blues of Tee-Tot's generation and the forms of R&B and soul that developed later, as well as the raw honky-tonk that Hank, Ernest Tubb and others sang. It was no surprise, given his Baby Boomer status, that he was a rocker at heart; during his teen years, he led a Nashville band known as Rockin' Randall & the Rockets. Growing increasingly irked about serving as Hank Lite, in 1967 (when he was 18), Audrey and MGM indulged him by allowing him to cut a rock single under another name, released on another label.

"Meter Reader Maid" and Bobby Darin's "Splish Splash," produced by R&B-rock producer Huey Meaux, was issued on the Verve label under the name Bocephus, the nickname Hank had

Hank Junior, ca. 1988

given him. While little more a throwaway, the disc hinted at Junior's future potential since he sang in his natural range. While "Meter Reader" suffered from a messy arrangement, "Splish," which was Darin by-the-numbers, presages "Mobile Boogie" and other later triumphs. He built on this by recording (under his own name) pleasant if bland early '70s covers of "Ain't That A Shame" and "Rainin' In My Heart" with the Mike Curb Congregation.

A form of Boomer gutbucket Hank couldn't have imagined became the true catalyst for Junior: the southern rock of the Allman Brothers, Charlie Daniels and Marshall Tucker bands. Embracing that sound would hasten the musical Armageddon between Junior and the sluggards at MGM. The culmination of that struggle was 1975's *Hank Williams Jr. And Friends*. With Vienneau out of the picture, Junior offered new, more personal originals with cameos from Charlie Daniels and the Marshall

Tucker Band's Toy Caldwell. A landmark achievement, the album reflected Junior's own mind and marked his turf, though exploiting it had to wait until after his lengthy recovery from his notorious, near-fatal spill off a Montana mountainside. By then, the bottle had claimed Audrey as well.

Junior's new sound and style resonated with his peers, most of them the sons and daughters of Hank fans. As a top concert draw and record seller, he savored his growing success by flipping off disapproval from the same Nashville establishment who'd coddled "Little Hank." Hanging with iconoclasts such as Johnny Cash, and prevailing in a creative conflict strikingly similar to the war won by his longtime pal Waylon Jennings, Junior created "Family Tradition," "Whiskey Bent And Hell Bound," and others that stand the test of time, even if his "Monday Night Football" theme is now what most people remember. The country edge, augmented with more blues and even jazz than Hank ever would have invoked, remained. Like Bob Wills, Junior jumped genres effortlessly, covering both Fats Waller's jazz standard "Ain't Misbehavin'" and Ernest Tubb's "Thanks A Lot."

Where did Hank's songs fit into all this? Junior never quit covering them, but his approach gained a more natural feel. In 1983 he joined Waylon, who'd staked his outlaw claim earlier with "Are You Sure Hank Done It This Way," for the Hank-themed hit "The Conversation." Junior's next-to-last #1 single was a cameo-laden "Mind Your Own Business." Then an old solo demo of Hank's ballad "There's A Tear In My Beer" resurfaced. With Junior's identity firmly established and Hank a cult figure, it was easy to clean up the audio and dub on a band and a duet vocal from Junior. Taking it to another, more contrived, level was the use of audio and video wizardry to sync "Tear" with Hank's 1952 TV performance of "Hey Good Lookin'" on "The Kate Smith Show" and blend Junior into the black-and-white video. It was a 1989 top-10 country hit, one overshadowed by the hype surrounding the creation of both the record and the video. And it was every bit as creepy as the earlier father-son efforts.

Hank's musical career ended abruptly; Junior's deteriorated more gradually, even as he inspired younger acts such as Montgomery Gentry and Travis Tritt. Watching him re-cover old ground and fall into the self-parody Hank avoided was painful. Even more pathetic were his half-assed, increasingly shrill attempts to convey his fist-shaking far-right politics, which were totally in sync with Music Row. Having recorded other singles in that vein, Junior hit his nadir during the 2008 presidential election when he demeaned "Family Tradition" by recasting it as a McCain-Palin campaign anthem. As the composer, he had every right to do it. Unfortunately, his "revised" lyrics, all GOP talking points, were so clumsy and out of meter they made "Raisin' McCain," John Rich's witless campaign anthem, seem poetic. Unveiling his "creation" at a McCain-Palin rally with both candidates present, the once-unassailable Bocephus stumbled through the tune like a drunk on karaoke night. But he did get to meet Sarah.

JETT Junior's half-sister Jett Williams is another matter. She grew up first with Lilly Williams (her grandmother), then was adopted into another family after Lilly's death, and it took time and years of court battles to establish her true heritage. But while Junior had to reject Daddy's shadow to find himself, Jett, who physically resembles her father, happily regurgitates his standards onstage, backed by a new version of the Drifting Cowboys that until their deaths, included original members Don Helms and Jerry Rivers. Does she do his music justice? Not really. Does she sound at ease with it? Nope. What's clear from hearing her is that her true vocal style, like that of her half brother, is rooted elsewhere. She owes as much, if not more, to Boomer blues icons Janis Joplin and Bonnie Raitt as she does to any country singer.

HANK III Jett looks like her father; Junior really doesn't. By contrast, Junior's son Shelton Hank, a.k.a. Hank III, eerily echoes his grandfather's visage. Beyond that, generational changes intervene. Hank III honors Hank by spearheading a futile attempt to restore him to the Opry roster that booted him in 1952 for his boozing. It's a noble effort, though in an era where the Opry settled a lawsuit with a living member (Stonewall Jackson) and smug, yuppified management seems bent on gutting the fading show's traditions, III's crusade has zero chance of success.

Hank III performing during SXSW, 2001. Photograph by John Carrico.

Like other Gen-Xers, Hank III would have no one tell him what to do or how to do it. With no Audrey to interfere and Hank Junior staying back, the onetime metal drummer would make his own mistakes, like locking himself into a long-term recording deal with Curb, an incompatible match given his musical duality: raw, unvarnished, often foulmouthed traditional country paired with his aggressive punk/metal side. He had little use for his 1999 debut album, *Risin' Outlaw*, which had only slight mainstream appeal. Nor did it take long for him to wind up in a legal battle, later settled, with Curb's squeaky-clean Republican mindset over his explicit recordings, a fight he publicized with a "Fuck Curb" campaign complete with T-shirts (they now release his recordings on the subsidiary label "Bruc"). It's safe to say that at their worst, neither Hank nor Junior would ever have sold "Fuck MGM" T-shirts.

One generational constant, however, remains. Like his ancestors, Hank III favors the gutbucket. For him that means a mix of old country, the late Jimmy Martin's style of bluegrass, the spirit of deceased punker GG Allin, the equally deceased Hasil Adkins and similar psychobilly acts. That's a matter of record. But a dichotomy emerges when it comes to traditional country. As much as he reveres Hank's music, III's take on it is equally colored by younger, Hank-inspired honky-tonkers, Wayne Hancock in particular but also Johnny Dilks and Dale Watson, all of whom III has praised. Contemptuous of mainstream fame, he enjoys an intense cult following, and while his hell-for-leather lifestyle reflects his ancestors, he views it and just about everything else through the eyes of his own age group.

HOLLY If Hank III's ties to his past seem muddled, half-sister Holly's are positively blurry. Born in 1981 and nearly a decade younger than III, she's a former model and interior designer who as a kid went to shows with her dad and only later discovered her grandfather's body of work. Given her comfortable upbringing, it's hardly surprising she can no more relate to the southern boogie of Junior's day than to the raw hymns Hank sang on the Mother's Best shows. Hank began in violent Alabama honky-tonks; Junior worked fancy auditoriums; Hank III plays punk clubs. Holly, who cites Leonard Cohen, Bob Dylan and Ron Sexsmith as influences, bears the spiritual imprint of Nashville's famed Bluebird Cafe, long-time proving ground for guitar-strumming singer-songwriters bent on joining that club's distinguished alumni.

For better or worse, she's the product of an even younger generation; their ties to the distant past changing and in many ways dissolving, regardless of lip service paid. While she

in many ways dissolving, regardless of lip service paid."

can, and has performed Hank's and Junior's material, *Here With Me*, her 2009 release on Mercury Nashville, was clearly aimed at mainstream-Americana success. At least one song, "Keep the Change," was geared to radio airplay. Beyond that, and the originals "Mama" and "Without

Jesus Here With Me" which reflect a distinct voice, she otherwise floats listlessly from one humorless ballad to the next, with no discernible style. At her worst, on the self-consciously arty "Three Days In Bed," she comes off much like Alison Krauss at her most pretentious. That doesn't mean she should follow Jett's lead and become Hank redux, which would ring false. Nor would it make sense to emulate Junior or her half-brother (I suspect she wouldn't handle III's "Thrown Out Of The Bar" very well). Sadly, there's little at this point to set her apart. Discussing her music on her website, she commented, "When it's in the blood, you can't help it." That's true, but when a Williams strives to sound too much like everyone else, one has to question to what degree it's in the blood at all.

Holly Williams performing at Joe's Pub, New York City, March 13, 2009. Photograph by Rahav Segev.

Even so, the Williams legacy, like the "country boy" Hank Junior once sang of, can and will survive about anything. With Hank, it's a given; half-asssed politics aside, Junior's music, too, will endure. Hank III is still evolving; Holly's off to an uncertain, less than promising start. Taken as a whole, their efforts are a microcosm of how succeeding generations, with their unique perspectives, view music. It's a view echoed in the controversial — but largely correct — essay on the end times for traditional country penned by *Newsweek* general editor Steve Tuttle in April 2009. At one point Tuttle declared, "Songwriters and hit makers write about what they know, just as their forefathers did, except now what they know is driving the kids to Target in the minivan..." True enough. And that ain't the Pan American, on her way to New Orleans.

Rich Kienzle, former ND *contributing editor, author of* Southwest Shuffle *(Routledge, 2003), and a music critic and historian since 1975, writes about country and jazz for various publications and does a weekly podcast for the* Pittsburgh Post-Gazette. *He still owns his first Hank Williams LP,* The Essential Hank Williams, *which he purchased in 1970 at the G.C. Murphy store in downtown Pittsburgh's Market Square.*

a complete service

COURTEOUS AND PROMPT

the REVIEWS appendix

GASOLINE, BUT NO MATCHES

NEIL YOUNG
Fork In The Road
(Reprise)

by GRANT ALDEN

LET US NOT succumb to bitterness, though that temptation lurks at the margins of everything these days. Or, as the prescient Merle Haggard sang bleakly and beautifully in 1982, the year I entered the work force full-time, "Are The Good Times Really Over?"

Let us, instead, talk about demographics, and fate. Neil Young, for example, was born in November of 1945, just before the dawn of the baby boom. He became an elder statesman who spoke to and for and about much of his generation, and mine. He was not simply present for Woodstock, he debuted his new band there. A hero, perhaps.

More than that, Young was and is a powerful, relentless creative force, yielding nothing to his years, a flickering beacon long before Emmylou Harris, Buddy Miller, Jon Dee Graham, or even Johnny Cash Himself would create work that argued compellingly for the durability of the artistic process across the barrier of middle age, and beyond.

It was Neil Young's generation which first grappled with and gave voice to the great social issues of the second half of the 20th century: race relations, Vietnam, women's rights, abortion, the (first) imperial presidency, ecology, gay rights. Young's curious adoption of Reaganism at the dawn of the 1980s is as emblematic of the decadence of that decade as anything (or reveals his creative process to be far more market-driven than a fan might wish to believe), for in that moment Boomers turned finally away from the promise of collective change and went quickly and viciously about the business of getting theirs.

Demographers have identified a second Baby Boom generation, born from 1954-65, and have labeled us — for I arrived in the middle — Generation Jones. As in keeping up with.

Well, we didn't.

Keep up with.

That this name is unsatisfactory and not a part of general discourse in the way our successors in Generations X and Y have entered the lexicon is fitting. Let me suggest, then, for my own age, a better name, a more accurate description: Generation Irrelevant.

(And, yes, I realize that our current president is an exemplar of my generation. I submit that he is an exception, in almost every way.)

Generation Irrelevant has faced no major forming, formative challenges, save how we might get by on the economic leavings of our elders. "Should I stay or should I go" was a great chant, and punk may have been our principal artistic legacy, but we were singing along with a song about sex, not about whether we should go to war or resist it. My lifelong pacifism has survived in the abstract, intact, even as now I learn to grow and perhaps to kill my own food.

More than a decade ago I interviewed an assortment of beatniks. One of them said, and this phrase has stuck with me ever since: "We took jobs for sport." In my lifetime there has never been a time when finding a job was easy. Never.

And so we waited, my cohorts in Generation Irrelevant, and at last we, too, succumbed to mortgages and children and 401(k) plans and all the rest, a little late getting there, a little behind our older brothers and sisters in the corner offices. Slaves to birth order, we waited our turn.

Except we don't get a turn. Or we missed

it. Or that was it, and it wasn't much, was it? Because the world now seems to be all about Generation Text, and what aps it can master; the world is all about new ways of ingesting information — playing with software — that bears no relationship to the world in which we were raised, and our skills...well, we're due for a bit of retraining, fit for a security uniform.

Again, those are not bitter words.

I do not mean to writhe in self-pity, for we have done our best, all of us. It just wasn't much, and we hoped for better. We hoped for a "Star Trek" future, and ended up with Los Lobos' "Is This All There Is?"

These are the bitter words, what nobody seems willing to say: We have known, at least since the 1970s, that the world would run out of oil, and that the planet was capable of sustaining a finite number of human beings. We have known, at least since the 1960s, that our activities on this planet were destroying it. And in the main, in all the ways which fundamentally matter, we have done nothing with this knowledge.

We have denied it, delayed it, debated it. (It was, in fact, the national high school debate topic of 1975-76, the year my partner and I finished thirteenth in the state of Washington.) We have settled for the most basic and rudimentary and painless kinds of remedies, as if the Clean Air Acts were enough, and not a beginning, not a carefully negotiated compromise designed to enrich rather than enrage the monied class. As if driving slightly lighter cars that get 20 miles a gallon instead of 10 miles a gallon were somehow sufficient. As if creating an economy built not on tangible things — which can be shipped across the ocean from places where nobody sees how and by whom they're made — but on unexplainable ephemeral notions were somehow a recipe for overcoming the considerable obstacles to survival we have not been facing.

We have done nothing. All of us. Me, too.

It is like this present Depression, which for the moment seems to have settled into a tolerable, manageable level of pain. We go on, day by day, as if the oil will last forever and climate change will somehow reverse itself with minimal effort, or not happen during our lifetime. As if our present economic dislocation were temporary. As if it were all going to be OK.

It isn't OK. It isn't going to *be* OK.

The recovery crowd learns to live one day at a time, and in that fashion to overcome the denial of their disease.

For the rest of us, that one step after another mantra leads to a more dangerous kind of denial, for it suggests that we are getting somewhere, rather than walking in circles.

By which circle we come 'round again to Mr. Young, and to his present work.

Young has most recently given us ten new songs more or less about cars and green fuel and, on the edges, about the changes we are all going through. Our anger. Why, then, are they delivered with such an absence of passion?

Neil Young has stayed more relevant longer than any artist of my lifetime. I have bought and listened to a great many of his records, quite at random, beginning on April 16, 1980, when I borrowed Scott Wayne's Honda because it was more dependable than my 1961 Ford F-100 pickup, and drove from Seattle to the Methow Valley of Washington state to report on a ski resort that was never built, to interview a man nicknamed Mr. Fun until several people were killed on a rafting trip his company ran.

Scott had an eight-track player, and a collection of tapes from the various members of Crosby, Stills, Nash & Young, including even Stills' *Thoroughfare Gap*, his 1978 foray into disco. But mostly I listened to Neil Young's 1979 *Live Rust*, and again and again to "Powderfinger" because it was, that day, my 21st birthday. And to "Needle And The Damage Done," but that's a family matter.

Neil Young would make a rockabilly record (hell, I bought John Lennon's rockabilly album, too, both of them in the cutout bins), would support Reagan, would record *Trans* and *Re-Ac-tor*, and would collaborate with Pearl Jam until it became a challenge to keep up, and then not necessary. Worth just staying in touch now and again, kinda like Facebook.

I have listened to *Fork In The Road* until I am tired of it, and it offers too little.

Maybe I need too much.

Maybe I no longer need.

Here is a central problem: Rock has a glorious subhistory of car songs. Robert Johnson's "Terraplane Blues," half of Chuck Berry's *oeuvre*,

Bobby Troup's "Route 66," the Beatles' "Baby You Can Drive My Car," Springsteen's "State Trooper." On and on. Those are gritty, industrial metaphors for sex and longing; they're quintessentially American songs about being trapped and running like hell, at least in one's imagination. These powerful, passionate, enduring songs, rooted in time and place...they're about freedom, in the end, aren't they?

Or, as Kris Kristofferson once would have it, "nothing left to lose."

Neil Young offers us a plateful of crunchy new songs about the machine itself, though the engineers have not made lovable cars for some decades. These new songs are rarely metaphorical, only occasionally revealing, and even the story "Johnny Magic" (about a self-taught mechanic, not a preternaturally gifted guitar player) is flat and didactic. They're about alternative fuels, these songs. Neil Young is a proponent of alternative fuels, vegetable oil and all the rest. Which is fine. Hell, it's a good thing, at least in theory, and it's a good thing to make a record about...right? But it all seems forced. A lecture.

It doesn't help that Jay Farrar's "When The Wheels Don't Move" (from the new Son Volt album, *American Central Dust*) gets it all said in a little over three minutes, filled with nuance and observation and taut emotion, and fierce guitar riffs. Neil Young should not suffer by comparison.

"Just singing a song/won't change the world," Young offers, with a swelling chorus behind him during "Just Singing A Song" (sigh), a world-weary repudiation of Graham Nash's "Chicago" ("We can change the world/Rearrange the world") that is meant as a call to action.

Yes, he can manage righteous anger, though "Cough Up The Bucks" owes too much to Faith No More's "We Care A Lot," and, anyway, isn't ten percent of James McMurtry's "We Can't Make It Here."

Past that, Young's advice is this: "Instead of cursing the darkness/Light a candle for where we're going," which sounds OK until the rest of "Light A Candle" segues into a facile kind of spirituality.

The best song probably is a toss-off, even though it's the title track. "I'm a big rock star," he sings. "My sales have tanked, but I've still got you." Even that leaves open the question whether he's talking to his wife, his friends, or his fans. "Keep on blogging, until the power goes out," he sings.

I guess that's something, but it's not enough.

SON VOLT
American Central Dust
(Rounder)

WITH A title evoking old desolations and new depressions, and a deceptively simple country-folk-rock aesthetic, the sixth Son Volt album would appear to cast a backward glance. But the music it contains and the twelve songs it collects are among the warmest and most inviting — one might say most present — that this band, and its singer and songwriter Jay Farrar, have ever released.

The inevitable comparison to 1995's *Trace* should be made only to be surpassed, as this is, of course, a very different Son Volt. Only Farrar remains, joined by the rhythm section of Andrew Duplantis and Dave Bryson (who signed up in 2005), Chris Masterson on electric guitar, and longtime friend Mark Spencer on a variety of instruments. Like *Trace*, the sound of the record is anchored by Farrar's acoustic guitar and voice, never stronger or more expressive, with Masterson and Spencer challenging each other on electric guitars, the rhythm section serving every song with a light touch, and the entire band contributing harmonies. Whereas *Trace* was obsessed with time, and the existential questions that arise from facing the clock, *American Central Dust* is obsessed with individual and collective survival — even as the levees break, roads turn to dust and the wheels grind to a standstill.

"When the levee goes, the heart breaks away" is the line that ignites "Dynamite," the album's opening track. The chorus, "This love is like celebrating the Fourth of July with dynamite," carried by close accordion and closer harmonies, is as near as Farrar has come to a pop hook since 2001's "Voodoo Candle," but the simile cuts in more than one way. Oddly, the song was not chosen as the first single; the second track, "Down To The Wire," received that designation. It's far denser, with drums recalling the rhythms of the *Wide Swing Tremolo* closer

"Blind Hope," Spencer's guitar sliding with psychedelic flourishes, and a chain of images that lay low all manner of modern institutions: "No jury will have the final say/Everyone knows the jury is guilty."

Farrar is too reflective for nihilism or solipsism, too smart and honest for nostalgia. The values he's sure will endure — the blues (even when it pushes a man too far), love (even when it could blow you to bits), language (even when elusive), dedication to a craft (even when the work gives little in return) — take on greater solidity and strength, because they are measured against the hardest recognitions. On "Dust Of Daylight," over a gorgeous country-rock arrangement straight out of the Gram Parsons songbook, Farrar looks at the future, making difficult predictions: "When you're lost in folly, out of luck in the worst of way/Love is a fog and you stumble every step you make." On "No Turning Back," a sweeping hymn to all traveling musicians, he chants a litany of towns and cities and praises "the salt and the steel of breath of those not keeping still." The band glides, weightless on whirling B3 and sparkling electric guitar.

And so the musical forms beat a retreat to a kind of traditionalism that Son Volt's previous album, *The Search*, explicitly reached beyond. It's a strategic retreat. Son Volt recorded the album in Farrar's St. Louis studio, then sent the tracks (for mixing) to Joe Henry, who lent the whole a transparent glow, and a subtle but clear personality that's inseparable from the underlying humanism of the songs. In that mix the songs cross over, luminous and mysterious, daring in their own way. The spare ballad "Sultana," for instance, dramatically evokes a Civil War-era disaster, "the Titanic of the cold Mississippi," in stark, factual lines. Farrar's piano just pounds chord after excruciating chord, and Eleanor Whitmore's fiddle cries out. The history sounds alive.

On another spare, piano-based ballad, "Cocaine And Ashes," Farrar, in a fairly rare move, inhabits the first-person voice of a character. Over piano and violin, he channels a hero, Keith Richards, and confides, "I have no pretensions of immortality/I've been told I have six months to live/But I've outlasted them all." And so will these songs. — **ROY KASTEN**

JOE HENRY
Blood From Stars
(Anti-)

JOE HENRY HAS made a few forays into film-scoring, and he seems like exactly the sort of tasteful auteur who will someday make a Randy Newman move into full-time soundtrack-composing. But that would be a real shame, and here's why: Henry already makes music so evocative and cinematic, visuals would almost be beside the point. *Blood From Stars*, Henry's eleventh album, is another very fine set of aural movies, and it just gets better and better the more plays you give it.

Two decades ago, it was by no means obvious that Henry was going to wind up in a place as cool as this. He started out as a mannered and not terribly distinguished singer-songwriter, making an awkward debut on 1986's conventional-to-a-fault *Talk Of Heaven*. His subsequent albums were better, and he uncorked a pair of twang-rock masterpieces in the early '90s — *Short Man's Room* (1992) and *Kindness Of The World* (1993), both recorded with the Jayhawks.

On those albums, Henry seemed to be perfectly positioned to capitalize on the dawn of the alternative-country era. But he chose a more idiosyncratic path and turned his back on convention with 1996's spacey *Trampoline*, which owed a lot more to Tom Waits (cool and urban) than to Uncle Tupelo (rural and hot). Since then, Henry's approach has evolved into an aesthetic based far more on atmosphere and texture than pop-song structure. You come away from his records remembering specific songs less than the overall mood and vibe.

Indeed, Henry has done his most accessible work over the past decade from behind the console, as go-to producer for venerable soul acts, among them Solomon Burke, Bettye LaVette and Allen Toussaint. Ani DiFranco, Ramblin' Jack Elliott, Loudon Wainwright III, Teddy Thompson, Mary Gauthier and many others have also benefited from Henry's deft production touch.

But Henry still finds (or makes) time to do an album of his own every couple of years. *Blood From Stars* is predictably eclectic, with jazz pianist Jason Moran, Waits guitarist Marc Ribot, and Henry's own son Levon (already a dynamite saxophonist at age 17) among the players. Henry arranges their contributions with meticulous care, in musical settings evocative enough to seem a lot less spare than they actually are.

With a prelude and a coda, *Blood From Stars* has an unusually formal structure. After the opening "Prelude: Light No Lamp When The Sun Comes Down" (rendered with skillful elan by pianist Moran), Henry makes his entrance in full-on character-actor mode on "The Man I Keep Hid," a piece of wise-guy vaudeville. Horns squawk, the piano weaves, and Henry barks like a carney. "Nobody knows...the man I keep hid," he drawls, the pause impeccably timed.

Yet you do feel like you've known this guy all your life, even if you're not quite sure what he's going on about. Henry narrates an obsessive series of apocalyptic ruminations, beautiful and poetic. Storms seem to figure prominently — "This Is My Cage" even invokes "the storm more perfect than peace" — leaving you to wonder if the blood from the title is meant to fall from the heavens like rain.

As has become typical for Henry, *Blood From Stars* is longer on ambience than accessibility. But there is one exception. "Channel" has the closest thing to a straight-up hook on the album, thunderously rolling along as stabs of piano pulse like lightning bolts. It's dreamy and powerful, each verse coming back to conclude with the same word:

> *I know the switch*
> *But keep the station*
> *I love you*
> *With all due desperation and disarray.*
> *Disarray...Disarray...Disarray.*

He makes disarray sound like the heaviest word ever. — **DAVID MENCONI**

IAN HUNTER
Man Overboard
(New West)

WHEN IAN HUNTER sang "The golden age of rock 'n' roll will never die" in 1974 with Mott The Hoople, he must have known that the era he celebrated was already long gone. Yet Hunter has always been tricky to read, the enigma behind the shades, with too much heart to be an ironist, too many smarts to be straightforward. When he sang "I Wish I Was Your Mother," he meant every tender sentiment of it, yet had to recognize the inherent humor of the very concept of the song. Just as when he wrote *Diary Of A Rock Star*, one of the best books ever about rock from the inside, he had to know he was hardly a star by rock's mega-standards, and that the inherent notion of rock stardom has a ludicrous dimension.

On his thirteenth solo studio album, there's only a bit of Mott — "I think I need another boost o' Mott The Hoople juice, yeah, I still got the legs," he sings on "Up And Running," a socially conscious class-warfare anthem — and only a slice of cautionary cynicism about rock stardom ("Ain't nothing worse than a phony-assed rebel," he sings on "Babylon Blues"). A follow-up of sorts to 2007's inspired *Shrunken Heads*, the eleven-cut song cycle finds Hunter and co-producer Andy York (guitarist for John Mellencamp) fashioning close-to-the bone arrangements for some of the richest, most moving and compelling music of Hunter's career.

Four decades after Mott The Hoople began (a milestone being celebrated with an October string of British reunion gigs) and 35 or so years after the band's semi-popular peak, "The Golden Age Of Rock 'N' Roll" is but a dim memory — maybe even a myth — yet Ian Hunter soldiers on, singing the good song, fighting the good fight. Though some of Hunter's early solo numbers ("Once Bitten, Twice Shy," "Cleveland Rocks") have had more staying power than most Mott music, it was Mott that provided Hunter with his musical identity, a populist frontman of Dylanesque phrasing with the Stones-style propulsion of the band.

Away from the band, Hunter sometimes seemed to lose his artistic bearings, chasing a hit, following whatever production/arrangement trend seemed to be in vogue, writing songs that tried too hard and rocked too little. So one of the things that impresses with his first album for New West — where the Brit transplant finds an Americana home — is just how comfortable he sounds in his own skin, how unforced this album is, how little it strains to impress.

The results sound simultaneously familiar and fresh, with no filler. York's banjo drives the picaresque romp of the album-opening "The

Great Escape," with one of Hunter's patented, exhilarating, sing-along choruses. (If Hunter were Rod Stewart — heaven forbid — this would be his "Every Picture Tells A Story"). Yet most of the highlights on an album full of them are the work of the mature balladeer. Hunter, who recently turned 70, always sounded older and wiser back in his Mott days, but rarely as tender and sage as this.

The combination of harpsichord delicacy and crass sentiment on "The Girl From The Office" results in the best Kinks song Ray Davies never wrote. The "drunk and disorderly" title ballad has a couplet for even the most sober-minded among us ("Reality this, reality that/I been there once and I ain't going back"). "Flowers" is metaphysical folk-rock at its deepest. "Win It All" is a secular hymn. Amid the Afrobeat pulse of "These Feelings," the artist affirms, "The spirit's still willing and the music always flows."

Flow on. Like fine wine, better with age.

— **DON MCLEESE**

BOOKER T.
Potato Hole
(Anti-)

POTATO HOLE is the first Booker T. Jones album in 15 years, and the consensus critical judgment is that it's a powerful effort, even a likely long-lister of the year's best. But the praise has been accompanied by a persistent caveat: Though featuring several way-cool Booker T. originals augmented by a couple of savvy covers (including Outkast's "Hey Ya"!), and despite co-starring Neil Young and the Drive-By Truckers, *Potato Hole* just never flames as brightly as the classic rock 'n' soul sides Jones cut with his fellow MG's for Stax Records in the 1960s and early '70s.

I think the consensus critical judgment is, for once, spot on. *Potato Hole* marks the successful artistic return of a soul music legend and all-around class-act. I hope it raises the curtain on another act in an already influential Hall of Fame career, the way *I Can't Stop* did for Al Green or *Don't Give Up On Me* did for Solomon Burke. And, beyond the man's indelible keyboard contributions as bandleader and sideman, this particular legend's return is welcome because

Jones is an accomplished albeit unheralded songwriter (he co-wrote "Big Bird" with Eddie Floyd, "Born Under A Bad Sign" with Albert King, and "Everyday Will Be Like A Holiday" with William Bell, among others), and a producer of masterpieces as diverse as Willie Nelson's *Stardust* and Bill Withers' *Just As I Am*.

And yet...every review of *Potato Hole* I've encountered posits some version of the same judgment: excellent record, just not nearly so excellent as those old ones. But why? What's different about it? None of the reviews say. *Potato Hole* just lacks some undefined indelible spark that was just oh-so unmistakably there in MG masterpieces such as "Green Onions," "Chinese Checkers" and "Time Is Tight."

Here's my theory: What the reviewers sense is missing on *Potato Hole* has everything to do with rhythm, particularly how the rhythm of any music shapes its use. Or, the other way round, how an audience expects to use music will be reflected in the music's rhythm. When Booker T. recorded with the MG's, job one was helping folks to dance — to "Shake," as Otis Redding put it.

Today, rock fans tap toes and nod heads (or even bang them), but mostly the expectation is that music is something to enjoy while sitting or standing, not dancing the night away. That's the world in which Neil Young has long thrived. And it's the approach of the Drive-By Truckers, a band that has always demonstrated a fairly rigid relationship to groove.

The DBTs' general avoidance of danceable grooves can seem unaccountable: Trucker Patterson Hood's dad, after all, played crowd-moving bass for Aretha Franklin and Wilson Pickett, and the band is famously in thrall to Lynyrd Skynyrd, whose own rhythms were born of boogie-woogie, western swing, and the blues — in other words, dance music.

But it's not unaccountable. Those dance-centric rock days are gone. This isn't a value judgment, understand, at least not entirely. There's more than one way to rock, and thank goodness. But I do think it's this relative lack of dance rhythm that critics are noticing when they say *Potato Hole* is missing...something. The whole rock scene is missing the same thing. And the absence never registers more than vaguely, because rock audiences no longer expect that something to be there in the first place.

So, on *Potato Hole*, Booker T. trades Cropper's resounding, stinging licks for Young's resounding, crunchy power chords. Less-is-more arrangements give way to layered sheets of sound, and instead of Al Jackson and Duck Dunn's fluid, just behind-the-beat grooves, we have the Truckers' heavy beats. The album's instrumental version of Tom Waits' "Get Behind The Mule" doesn't swing or sway; per its title, it plods. And in the scorching "Native New Yorker," the Manhattanite in question is definitely not taking the A-Train.

Of course, Booker T. knows who he's playing for, now. Those great old MG's records often had dance-suggestive names such as "Soul Limbo," "Groovin'," "Can't Be Still" and "Hip Hug-Her." But the opening keyboard on *Potato Hole* is quickly swallowed alive by Young's power-chording and the Truckers' thundering straight-up-and-down drums. The song's called "Pound It Out." — **DAVID CANTWELL**

LARRY JON WILSON
self-titled
(Drag City)

"IT AIN'T A marshmallow song," says Larry Jon Wilson at the conclusion of "Where From," the fatalistic, life-spanning ballad that is the last track of his self-titled new album. And if a work of art can be fairly judged in the negative, then let it be said that Wilson's first album in nearly three decades is chock-full of songs that ain't marshmallow songs.

A songwriter who first achieved notice as a charter member of Nashville's bohemian outlaw poets in the 1970s (he was signed to Monument Records by Fred Foster, who rendered a similar service to Kris Kristofferson), Wilson released four albums and labored for a decade in the Music City vineyards before calling it quits. Now he's back on his own terms, with an intimate acoustic performance that is as close as listeners will ever come to sampling Wilson's presence at a guitar pull in their own living room.

Recorded on the fifteenth floor of a condo tower in Perdido Key, on the Florida/Alabama state line, the album finds Wilson armed with just an acoustic guitar and some sympathetic

ears in the form of producers/fans Jeb Loy Nichols and Jerry DeCicca, and engineer Jake Housh. (The tasty fiddle that gilds several of the tracks was recorded later.) Sessions were scheduled in between gigs and many cocktails and fried-fish entrees.

After decades of toil, Wilson's voice has been burnished to a weathered, whiskeyed thing, akin to the "age-before-beauty" tones of fellow travelers such as Guy Clark, Jesse Winchester and Mickey Newbury. Indeed, Wilson covers two Newbury tracks, "Bless The Losers" and "Frisco Mabel Joy," as part of a pair of medleys (the "Loser's Trilogy" and the "Whore's Trilogy," respectively).

It's evident from his original material and his choice of covers that Wilson feels a certain kinship with whores, losers, and others on life's fringes. In his own "Things Ain't What They Used To Be," he asks, "If she won't leave me when I'm down/How's she ever gonna go?" His cover of Willie Nelson and Bob Dylan's "Heartland" laments "a hole in my chest where my heart used to be" and "a hole in the sky where God used to be." And he compares an abandoned lover to "A symphony with no strings/An eagle with no wings/A sapphire without blue."

The sentiments are amplified by the intimacy of the performances. Wilson's fingers squeak against the strings, and his knuckles rap the body of the guitar. At one point, he grumbles about the noise from the air conditioner and the ice machine in the hall. There's a sense that he's playing as much for himself as (to paraphrase *Sunset Boulevard*) those people out there in the dark.

In a world of "American Idol" and "Nashville Star," Wilson knows he's nobody's idea of the Next Big Thing, and he's OK with that. He takes Fort Worth rocker Bruce Channel's playful "Rocking Chair" and makes it his steady-rolling own: "That old rocking chair don't scare me like it used to," he sings with the hard-won assurance of age, "as long as I'm rockin' with you."

It's not all working girls and downbeat drifters, by any means. "Long About Now" and "Feel Alright Again" both glide along on thoughts of loving arms and better days, and "I Am No Dancer" is a lovely tone poem of light feet and lifted hearts. But there is a gravity to the balance of the album that keeps it grounded in the hardscrabble day-to-day, and in the ways people make peace with dreams that have gone around the bend. **— JOHN T. DAVIS**

WILCO
Wilco (The Album)
(Nonesuch)

BASEBALL IS the enduring American metaphor for, well, just about everything. And in 2002, when I spoke to Jay Bennett about his last days as guitarist, keyboardist and songwriter with Wilco, he defaulted to the field of dreams.

When Bennett was a youngster, baseball was his life (he was a shortstop and catcher), and he loved the game obsessively. Then one season his team got a new coach whose manner and style snuffed out his enthusiasm for baseball. Bennett went from relishing every practice to quietly hoping for a cancellation due to rain. Years later, as his tenure with Wilco fizzled to an end, he said he was consumed with that same feeling when he was preparing to tour or record: I hope this gets rained out.

I recalled this sporting metaphor from Bennett, who died on May 24, when I was preparing to listen to Wilco's seventh album (or tenth if you include a live record and two Billy Bragg *Mermaid Avenue* collaborations). It's hard to recall the anticipation with which I once greeted a new Wilco album. This time, wary of my waning affection for their music, I caught myself thinking…rain delay?

Wilco (The Album) has its moments. The graceful "Solitaire" pairs one of Jeff Tweedy's more morose, reflective lyrics ("Once I thought without a doubt/I had it all figured out/Universe with hands unseen/I was cold as gasoline") to a pillowy bed of organ, electric piano, acoustic guitar and subliminal drum work from Glenn Kotche. "Sonny Feeling" is AOR radio-ready for 1976 with a strange time-jumping lyric and a chorus ("The sunny feeling is taken away!") that belies the buoyancy of the song.

That strategy of contrast is applied with lesser returns on "You Never Know," which gives voice to the cynicism of an older generation toward the young folks' activism ("C'mon children,

you're acting like children/Every generation thinks it's the end of the world") and pairs it with a melody and guitar part that echo George Harrison's "My Sweet Lord." "Wilco (The Song)" amusingly co-opts the rhetoric of late-night TV commercials to boast of the band's prowess, like they were the audio equivalent of the Sham-Wow or Slanket. But the needling staccato piano riff of "Bull Black Nova" is dental surgery applied to the ears, notwithstanding Kotche's heroic attempts to make something lively out of it. The vaunted summit of Tweedy and Leslie Feist on "You And I" passes without disturbance; is it just me, or does this sound like a slightly slower version of America's "Sister Golden Hair"? The thoughtful verses of "I'll Fight," which seems to allude to the class-based inequity of military service, are sabotaged by an unworthy, simplistic, repetitive chorus. Wilco used to be better than this.

The very theme of the album seems to be the duality of change — timely, given that a U.S. election was won on the optimism that change can inspire. But Tweedy's songs also seem to acknowledge that change requires courage or ruthlessness in breaking with the past. My growing estrangement from Wilco's sound is not because of some desire for artistic stasis. I like my artists to follow a quixotic path. Yet Wilco's recent concert DVD, *Ashes Of American Flags*, chockablock as it is with musical climaxes tediously resolved by a succession of guitarist Nels Cline's whammy-bar freakouts, reinforced the notion that change in itself is not a value; it's where you end up that matters.

But things do change. It's true of musicians and music fans, too. It's a point Tweedy himself voices on the very fine "One Wing" ("This is what happens when we separate/This is what happens to all dead weight, eventually") and with somewhat less grace on the overstuffed album-closer "Everlasting Everything":

Everything alive must die,
Every building built to the sky
Don't try to tell me my everlasting love
*   is a lie*

Wilco is still capable of making some fine music, but *Wilco (The Album)* is a test of unqualified ardor.

— PAUL CANTIN

VARIOUS ARTISTS
The Man Of Somebody's Dreams:
A Tribute To The Songs Of Chris Gaffney
(Yep Roc)

WHEN CHRIS GAFFNEY was diagnosed with liver cancer ion 2008, Dave Alvin began putting together *A Man Of Somebody's Dreams* to raise funds for his treatment. Gaffney's death within just a few weeks of his diagnosis turned the project into a tribute, and a keystone of Alvin's personal mission to elevate his sideman and best friend's music from obscurity.

Gaffney's band performed regularly in California bars and clubs, and he released six records from 1986 through 1999. His music knew few genre boundaries. What it all had in common was a hard-to-resist invitation to cry, to laugh, or to dance two-step, Norteño, jitterbug, polka or punk pogo. His 1995 disc *Loser's Paradise* incorporated an all-star cast of friends and admirers, including Alvin, the Small Faces' Ian McLagan, Austin accordionist Ponty Bone, Jim Lauderdale, Lucinda Williams, Rosie Flores, and Dale Watson.

More recently, Gaffney had teamed with Dave Gonzales (of erstwhile rockabilly outfit the Paladins) in the Hacienda Brothers. They debuted promisingly in 2005 with an eponymous release produced by R&B legend Dan Penn, who also produced the band's 2006 disc *What's Wrong With Right*. The band's third Penn-produced album, *Arizona Motel*, was released two months after Gaffney died.

In his liner notes to *A Man Of Somebody's Dreams*, Alvin ponders why Gaffney's career had not found more success. He cites "downright cruel rejection letters from Nashville A&R folks" and "cold indifference from the trend-obsessed pop/rock world." And he speculates that "one reason for his lack of mainstream success was that...Chris was influenced by everything he heard, from the borderland Mexican music to the country, R&B and rock and roll on jukeboxes and AM radio."

Alvin's tribute reflects that sprawling aesthetic with 21 contributing acts, including many old friends and some that Gaffney never knew. Alvin plays on several tracks, as do longtime Gaffney sidemen Wyman Reese and Danny Ott. Alvin's own entry, "Artesia," opens with a poetic reverie of semi-rural 1960s California, as he and Gaffney knew it growing up. "Artesia" is story-song, with characters that could as easily have been created by Butch Hancock. The chorus captures the loss of that era: "Now when the wind blows/From out of Artesia/I can't smell 1965."

Gonzales sings Gaffney's old-time rock 'n' roller "So Tired To Be Me" with Ponty Bone on accordion. Penn renders the soul-filled "I'm So Proud" with phrasing almost identical to Gaffney's version. (Who influenced whom?) It was the first song the Hacienda Brothers wrote together. Another highlight is "The Gardens," which first appeared on the Texas Tornados' 1996 album *4 Aces*. Freddy Fender sings lead vocals, Doug Sahm sings harmony and plays guitar, and Ry Cooder sits in.

Gaffney's fellow Californians John Doe and Boz Scaggs render "Quiet Desperation" and "Midnight Dream," respectively, with Los Lobos taking on the title track. Peter Case sings the memorable Alvin/Gaffney co-write "Six Nights A Week," and Lauderdale delivers Gaffney's certifiable country weeper "Glass House," backed by Ollabelle. Other contributors — Joe Ely, Tom Russell, James McMurtry, Big Sandy & Los Straitjackets, Alejandro Escovedo, Robbie Fulks — are artists you'd expect to make the most of a Gaffney song. Calexico is more of a surprise; to make it work, they wrote new music for "Franks Tavern," a song about one of Gaffney's favorite watering holes in South Tucson.

The tribute concludes with the one thing that haunts the record by its absence: the sound of Gaffney's own indelible, soulful voice. He sings not his own song, but a cover, written by Stanley Wycoff and Michael Berberet of the micro-obscure and bizarre early '90s band Bierce In LA. It's the last song Gaffney recorded, when he knew he had cancer, and it's called "Guitars Of My Dead Friends."
— **LINDA RAY**